Contents

A Message to Parents / 9

Introduction: Get Cooking! / 11

Safety in the Kitchen / 15

Commonly Used Cooking Terms / 18

Spring / 20

Summer / 58

Fall / 98

Winter / 134

Index / 174

Little Kenny

in the

Kitchen

Ken Kostick Cooks for Kids

Illustrations by Jon McKee

KEY PORTER  BOOKS

National Library of Canada Cataloguing in Publication Data

Kostick, Ken, 1954-
    Little Kenny in the kitchen : Ken Kostick cooks for kids/Ken Kostick.

Includes index.
ISBN 1-55263-499-X

1. Cookery—Juvenile literature. I. Title.

TX652.5.K67 2002   j641.5'123   C2002-903004-8

The publisher gratefully acknowledges the support of the Canada Council for the Arts and the Ontario Arts Council for its publishing program.

We acknowledge the financial support of the Government of Canada through the Book Publishing Industry Development Program (BPIDP) for our publishing activities.

Key Porter Books Limited
70 The Esplanade
Toronto, Ontario
Canada M5E 1R2

www.keyporter.com

Design: Peter Maher
Electronic formatting: Heidi Palfrey

Printed and bound in Canada

02 03 04 05 06 5 4 3 2 1

I would like to dedicate this book
to all my four-legged friends.

They bring us unconditional
love and support.

A Message to Parents

Little Kenny in the Kitchen is a wonderful way to introduce your children to the magic of cooking. In the pages that follow, they'll accompany Little Kenny, his three dogs and his mother, Helen, on a journey through the kitchen—a journey that focuses on health, safety and, above all, fun. They'll learn how to make more than 70 delicious, healthy meals and snacks. They'll be introduced to kitchen basics like cleanliness and safety, and they'll become familiar with dozens of general cooking terms and procedures. In the end, they'll emerge with a new respect for and fascination with the process of food preparation. Don't be surprised if you're presented with breakfast in bed on your next birthday!

This book was meticulously prepared with your child's safety in mind. As you read the introductory pages, you'll find a comprehensive section on safety in the kitchen. You'll also learn that Little Kenny's mother is always on hand as an "adult helper." Each recipe contains instructions about what Little Kenny's mother does to help out—from turning on the stove and removing items from the oven to chopping fruits and vegetables. This segment is designed to prompt your child to ask for help. Before getting started, however, it may be a good idea to go over your own rules for the kitchen. It's up to you and your child to determine what's permissible and what's not.

I hope you enjoy using *Little Kenny in the Kitchen* as much as I enjoyed writing it. It's my hope that it will encourage a new generation of great chefs to get out there and start cooking. When a little creativity combines with a lot of fun, the results are always spectacular!

—*Ken Kostick*

Introduction: Get Cooking!

If you could make your own food, would you have cookies for breakfast and ice cream for lunch? Would dinner be homemade macaroni and cheese, or popcorn? What's stopping you? Cooking doesn't have to be hard—and it doesn't have to be all about snacks, either. With just a little help and the right ingredients, you can work magic in the kitchen!

In *Little Kenny in the Kitchen* you'll find more than 70 tasty, fun to make, fun to eat recipes. Each can be completed in three easy steps, with simple ingredients that you'll be able to find in your own kitchen. And unless the recipe calls for baking, you'll be able to complete it in less than half an hour.

Meet the Chefs

Before you head for the kitchen and tie on that apron, let's meet the characters that will help you out. First, there's Little Kenny. Kenny's a kid who loves to cook. In between doing other kid stuff (like going to school, playing baseball, and hanging out with his friends), Kenny creates recipes that taste good and are easy for anyone to make—even an adult!

Although Little Kenny is a terrific cook, he still needs help from time to time. Luckily, Kenny's mom is always around (you can call her **Helen**). Whenever Little Kenny's in the kitchen, Helen is nearby, ready to lend a helping hand.

Little Kenny's mom isn't the only one helping him out. Kenny's three faithful dogs—Benny, Pearl and Napoleon—are always nearby. All three love food, and are constantly underfoot, cleaning up after Kenny if he drops something on the floor!

Benny's a big, black schnauzer who loves to play. His favorite game is catch, but even Kenny won't let him play in the kitchen. Because he needs to watch his weight—he's 110 pounds!—Benny's become an expert on nutrition. He's always interrupting Kenny in the middle of cooking to point out healthier ways to prepare the food. Helen loves Benny.

Pearl is a white boxer. She's very smart—which can be a bit annoying at times. All that knowledge is handy, though, when it comes to changing recipes around. For example, Kenny wouldn't have known that Helen's Easy Strawberry Pie could become Helen's Easy Peach Pie unless Pearl had told him. This is handy information—especially if you hate strawberries!

Napoleon is Little Kenny's chihuahua. Because he's a small dog (he only weighs five pounds, which means he has to be careful not to get stepped on by Benny!), Napoleon can go almost anywhere with Kenny. He's stayed at hotels and been on more planes than some people! All that traveling has made Napoleon the king of trivia. The other dogs get bored listening to him go on, but his hints and tips are really interesting. It was Napoleon who told Kenny that oranges were first grown in China, and that the strawberry is actually related to the rose! Who knew?

How to Use This Book

As you look through the recipes that follow, you'll find some that are perfect for family dinners, many that are great for parties with your friends, and others that will make terrific treats just for yourself. Part of the fun of cooking is in planning—choosing just the right recipe for you, your family or your guests—and Little Kenny and his furry friends have made sure to give you enough information to plan well.

To help you sort out the really easy recipes from the ones that will take a little more time, the dogs have come up with the bone rating system. On the "bone scale," one bone is the easiest, two bones indicate a recipe of medium difficulty, and three bones tell you that things might be a little harder. If you only have a little bit of time to spend in the kitchen, look for a one-bone recipe; if you're planning a surprise for your father's birthday, you might want to try a three-bone specialty!

Each recipe in this book also lets you know what your helper should be doing. Little Kenny likes his mother to do most of the chopping, drain the pasta, heat up the oven, and handle dishes going in and out of the oven. She also turns on the stove and manages the heat level. As Little Kenny gets older he will learn do some of the preparation—like chopping—safely. The sections called "Little Kenny's Mother" that accompany each recipe will show you where you need help. (For more tips on Safety in the Kitchen, see page 15.)

Little Kenny's mother is also helpful when it comes to grocery shopping. Before you begin to cook, it's important to make sure that you have all of the ingredients you'll need. Look at the recipe's ingredient list and then poke around your kitchen. If you're missing something, make a list. When your list is complete, ask someone to take you to the supermarket. Little Kenny has made sure that the ingredients his recipes call for are easy to find. You don't need anything fancy. When shopping, always look for fresh ingredients, and reads labels if you buy anything in a can. If the product has ingredients that you can't pronounce, you might want to try another brand.

One last tip: Whenever he's cooking, Little Kenny prefers to have all of his ingredients set up near the stove before he starts. Try it at your house. It's easier and more fun to cook when everything's right where you need it.

Safety in the Kitchen

Cooking is fun, but it can also be dangerous if some basic safety rules aren't followed. On the next two pages, you'll find important information on safety in the kitchen. Read it yourself and then ask your adult helper to read it, too. If you have any questions, ask your helper to explain. The same goes for while you're cooking. It doesn't matter if you're smack in the middle of a recipe: if you come across something confusing, or something that you're not sure you should be doing, stop and ask. Safety should always come first.

Ovens

Ovens can get extremely hot! Because of this, you should always ask an adult to supervise when a recipe calls for oven use. Here are some additional tips for safe oven use:

- Ask your adult helper to preheat the oven for food that needs baking or broiling.
- Ask your adult helper to take the dishes in and out of the oven.
- Arrange the oven racks before the oven is turned on—you won't have to change the racks around when things begin to heat up.
- Turn on the oven light so that you can watch your food without opening the oven door.
- If you do have to open the door, take a step back before reaching for your dish. This will allow the hot steam to escape.

The Stove Top

Like ovens, stove tops can get hot—but there's no door in the way to protect your hands. Keep the following tips in mind when cooking on top of the stove.

- Ask your adult helper to turn the element on and adjust it to the right heat level. If the heat level needs to be changed during cooking, ask your adult helper to do this as well. If you and your helper have agreed that it's okay for you to operate the elements, it still makes sense to have him or her nearby.
- When using a pot, wok, sauté pan, or grill pan, always turn the handles to the side of the stove top to avoid knocking or tipping. Not only is the stove top hot, the food in the pot is hot, too!
- If you are cooking with more than one dish, make sure that pot handles are not sitting over top of the next element. You could burn yourself when you pick up the pot.
- Do not leave any cooking tools—like wooden spatulas, ladles or spoons—on the side of the stove. They could get hot or even burn.
- Do not wear loose clothing that could rest on an element and catch on fire.

Appliances

Food processors, blenders, and mixers are all important when it comes to food preparation. Since these are all electric appliances, though, certain precautions need to be taken.

- Make sure that your hands and the counter top are dry before plugging an appliance in. If you're not sure if conditions are safe, ask your adult helper.

- If something needs to be puréed, make sure it's cool before pouring it into the blender or food processor. Ask your adult helper to make sure the lid is on properly before pressing the buttons.

Kitchen Basics

In the kitchen, being clean is almost as important as being safe. Always wash your hands before you begin to cook, and try to clean up your spills and dribbles as you go along (it will save you from a big cleanup at the end!). On his show, Little Kenny finds that keeping a wet cloth or paper towel nearby helps with messy situations.

Keeping yourself clean can also be tricky! Little Kenny always wears an apron to help keep his clothes neat. He's also learned to tie a towel to the apron for those many occasions when he needs to wipe his hands.

When you're finished in the kitchen, wash your cutting boards with soapy water, and put all of the dishes in the dishwasher or the sink. Then, take off your apron, throw it in the laundry basket and give your hands one last wash.

Commonly Used Cooking Terms

Bake

To cook in an oven at preheated temperature using the middle rack.

Blend

To mix together specific ingredients.

Boil

To heat a liquid to a high point where it bubbles.

Chill

To refrigerate until a cool temperature is reached.

Chop

To cut the ingredient into small pieces.

Combine

To put two or more ingredients together.

Dice

To cut into small 1/4 inch pieces, square shaped.

Drain

To strain away any liquid.

Garnish

To decorate food.

Grate

To run an ingredient like cheese or a vegetable down the side of a grater until you collect the right amount.

Grease

To grease a pan or baking dish, pie plate, or cookie sheet with low-fat spray or margarine so that the batter will not stick.

Melt

To heat solid food until it has turned into liquid.

Peel

To take off the outer layer of fruit or vegetable with a sharp knife.

Purée

To mix ingredients together using a food processor or hand blender until smooth.

Sauté

To cook food quickly in oil or another liquid in a frying pan, sauté pan, or wok.

Simmer

To soak a liquid at a temperature just below the boiling point.

Stir

To mix two or more ingredients in a circular motion.

Stir-fry

To quickly fry food in a wok or large sauté pan on high, constantly stirring.

Whisk

To mix ingredients together from side to side with a metal whisk.

Spring

Carrot and Bran Muffins with Raisins / 22

Little Kenny's Hotcakes / 24

Fruit Pizza on Pita / 24

Spinach and Pear Salad with Feta / 28

Spring Carrot and Orange Salad / 30

Little Kenny's Easy Tomato and Rice Soup / 32

Spring Vegetable Soup with Fresh Parsley / 34

Very Creamy Cream of Corn and Potato Soup / 36

The Best Western Sandwich with Herbs / 38

Portobello Mushroom Pizza with Red Pepper / 40

Mother's Day Four-Cheese Rice and Broccoli / 42

Mushroom Helper with Pasta and Cheese / 44

Spaghetti Squash Curry / 46

Green Stir-fry with Basil / 48

Spring Vegetables and Fusilli with Parmesan / 50

Little Kenny's Pad Thai / 52

Incredible Peanut Butter Cookies / 54

Little Kenny's Unbelievable Chocolate Chip Cookies / 56

Carrot and Bran Muffins with Raisins

1 3/4 cups	bran cereal	425 mL
1 1/2 cups	flour	375 mL
1 cup	sugar	250 mL
2 tsp	baking powder	10 mL
1/2 tsp	cinnamon	2 mL
3	medium carrots, grated	3
1/2 cup	raisins	125 mL
1	large egg, beaten	1
3/4 cup	milk	175 mL
2/3 cup	vegetable oil	160 mL

Bone Rating:

Makes: 12 regular muffins or 24 mini muffins

Preparation Time: 10 minutes

Cooking Time: 15 minutes

Cookware: Large and medium mixing bowls, nonstick 12-muffin regular tin or 24-muffin mini-muffin tin

1. In the large bowl, combine the dry ingredients and mix well. Stir in the carrots and raisins.

2. In the medium bowl, blend together the egg, milk and oil. Add the egg mixture to the dry mixture and combine them well.

3. Spoon the batter into the muffin tins, filling each cup about half full. Bake the muffins in a preheated oven at 400°F (200°C) for 15 minutes, or until a toothpick inserted in the middle of a muffin comes out clean.

Replace the raisins with chopped dates.

Little Kenny's mother preheats the oven and helps him grate the carrots.

Little Kenny trades mini muffins with his friends at school for good stuff.

Little Kenny's Hotcakes

Add 1/2 cup (125 mL) fresh blueberries to make blueberry pancakes.

Bone Rating:

Makes: About 10 pancakes

Preparation Time: 10 minutes

Cooking Time: 15 minutes

Cookware: 2 medium mixing bowls, large sauté pan

1 cup	flour	250 mL
1 tbsp	granulated sugar	15 mL
1 tbsp	baking powder	15 mL
1/4 tsp	baking soda	1 mL
1/4 tsp	cinnamon (optional)	1 mL
1	large egg	1
1 cup	buttermilk	250 mL
2 tbsp	olive oil	30 mL
2 tbsp	butter	30 mL

To lower the fat content of this recipe, use skim milk instead of buttermilk and margarine instead of butter.

Hotcakes have different names—pancakes, flapjacks or griddle cakes—and are usually served with maple syrup.

Little Kenny's mother helps him cook the pancakes.

1 In one bowl, combine the flour, sugar, baking powder, baking soda and cinnamon (if using). Stir well.

2 In the other bowl, combine the egg, buttermilk and olive oil and whisk together. Add the egg mixture to the flour mixture and stir until the batter has no lumps.

3 Melt the butter in the sauté pan on medium heat until the butter bubbles. Pour a large spoonful of the batter into the pan. Cook until the pancake is golden brown, turn it with a spatula and cook the other side. Keep the cooked pancakes warm in the oven while you cook the others.

Fruit Pizza on Pita

1	pita bread	1	
2 tbsp	peanut butter	30 mL	
1	small apple, cored and sliced	1	
1	small pear, cored and sliced	1	
1/2 cup	chopped pineapple	125 mL	
1/2 cup	goat cheese (optional)	125 mL	

1 Place the pita bread on the baking sheet and spread the bread evenly with the peanut butter. Place the fruit on top. Sprinkle with the cheese (if using).

2 Bake in a preheated oven at 325°F (160°C) for 10 to 12 minutes, or until the edges of the pita start to brown. Cut in half and serve.

Little Kenny's mother preheats the oven and helps him core and slice the apple and pear and chop the pineapple.

Bone Rating:

Makes: 2 servings

Preparation Time: 10 minutes

Cooking Time: 10 to 12 minutes

Cookware: Baking sheet

Little Kenny likes to make this pita pizza as an after-school snack for all of his friends.

Replace the peanut butter with jam or even maple syrup.

Spinach and Pear Salad with Feta

Bone Rating: 🦴
Makes: 4 servings
Preparation Time:
10 minutes
Cookware: Medium and small mixing bowls

1	medium pear, cored and thinly sliced	1
2 tbsp	lemon juice	30 mL
4 cups	chopped baby spinach	1 L
1/2 cup	crumbled feta cheese	125 mL
1/4 cup	chopped walnuts	60 mL
1/4 cup	olive oil	60 mL
3 tbsp	apple cider vinegar	45 mL
1 tbsp	brown sugar	15 mL

Replace the feta with a mild goat cheese.

Spinach was brought to North America from Spain. Spinach, which is a good source of iron, is wonderful in salads or soups. When spinach is used in certain dishes, they are referred to as "Florentine," which in French means "in the style of Florence" (a city in Italy).

1. In the medium bowl, coat the pear with the lemon juice to keep the pear from browning.

2. Arrange the spinach, pear, feta and walnuts evenly on 4 side or salad plates.

3. In the small bowl, whisk together the olive oil, vinegar and brown sugar to make a dressing. Drizzle the dressing evenly on top of the salads.

Little Kenny's mother helps him core and slice the pear and chop the spinach and walnuts.

To lower the fat content of this recipe, use low-fat feta or even low-fat mozzarella or Parmesan cheese.

Spring Carrot and Orange Salad

Bone Rating: 🦴🦴

Makes: 4 servings

Preparation Time:
  15 minutes

Cookware: Medium and
  small mixing bowls

The carrot is a member of the parsley family. A popular vegetable year-round, carrots can be cooked in a variety of dishes, or even in baked goods.

2	medium seedless oranges, peeled and chopped	2
2 cups	grated carrot	500 mL
1/2 tsp	dried mint	2 mL
	or	
1 tbsp	chopped fresh mint	15 mL
1/4 cup	mayonnaise	60 mL
1/4 cup	orange juice with pulp	60 mL
1/4 cup	plain yogurt	60 mL
1/4 cup	chopped fresh parsley	60 mL

❶ In the medium bowl, combine the orange, carrot and mint and mix well.

❷ In the small bowl, combine the mayonnaise, orange juice and yogurt and blend well.

❸ Pour the mayonnaise mixture in with the carrot mixture and mix. Top with the fresh parsley.

Replace the mint with tarragon.

Little Kenny's mother helps him chop the oranges, mint and parsley and grate the carrots.

To lower the fat content of this recipe, use low-fat mayonnaise and low-fat or nonfat yogurt.

31

Little Kenny's Easy Tomato and Rice Soup

Bone Rating:

Makes: 4 to 6 servings

Preparation Time:
   10 minutes

Cooking Time: 15 minutes

Cookware: Large pot

1	can (28 oz/796 mL) diced tomatoes	1
2	stalks celery, chopped	2
1	small green bell pepper, chopped	1
1	small onion, chopped	1
1 1/2 cups	tomato juice	375 mL
3/4 cup	long-grain white rice	175 mL
1/2 tsp	black pepper	2 mL
1/2 tsp	dried basil	2 mL
	or	
1 tbsp	chopped fresh basil	15 mL
1/2 tsp	sea salt	2 mL
1/2 cup	chopped fresh parsley	125 mL

Little Kenny always tries to use what is at the local supermarket.

Canned tomatoes are a quick and easy ingredient to use in soups and a lot of other dishes, such as pasta sauces and stews.

1 Combine all of the ingredients in the pot, except the parsley. Bring the mixture to a boil on high heat, reduce the heat to medium and simmer for 15 minutes, stirring constantly.

2 Add the parsley and serve immediately.

Little Kenny's mother helps him chop the celery, bell pepper, onion, fresh basil and fresh parsley.

You can add 1 cup (250 mL) cooked rice to this soup, which is a good way to use up leftover rice.

Spring Vegetable Soup with Fresh Parsley

For a different flavor, replace the fresh parsley with fresh coriander.

Add other vegetables that you li[ke] or that you might have left ove[r]

Bone Rating:

Makes: 6 servings

Preparation Time: 10 minutes

Cooking Time: 15 minutes

Cookware: Large pot

1/2 cup	vegetable stock or apple juice	125 mL
2	cloves garlic, chopped	2
2	stalks celery, chopped	2
1	medium carrot, chopped	1
1	small onion, chopped	1
1	small red bell pepper, chopped	1
1	can (28 oz/796 mL) diced tomatoes	1
1	medium potato, peeled and diced	1
5 cups	vegetable stock	1.25 L
1/2 tsp	black pepper	2 mL
1/2 tsp	dried thyme	2 mL
	or	
1 tbsp	chopped fresh thyme	15 mL
1/2 tsp	sea salt	2 mL
1/2 cup	chopped fresh parsley	125 mL

Little Kenny's mother helps him chop the garlic, celery, carrot, onion, bell pepper, thyme and parsley and dice the potato.

To lower the fat content of this recipe, use low-fat vegetable stock.

1 In the pot, heat the vegetable stock or apple juice on medium heat and gently sauté the garlic, celery, carrot, onion and red bell pepper for about 3 to 4 minutes.

2 Add all of the other ingredients, except the parsley, and bring the mixture to a boil on high heat. Reduce the heat to medium and simmer the soup for 12 to 15 minutes.

3 Add the parsley and serve immediately.

Very Creamy Cream of Corn and Potato Soup

Bone Rating: 🦴🦴

Makes: 6 servings

Preparation Time:
   10 minutes

Cooking Time: 20 minutes

Cookware: Large pot,
   hand blender

Replace the Dijon mustard with 1 tsp (5 mL) mild curry powder, which will give a nice yellow color and added flavor.

2	cloves garlic, chopped	2
2	large potatoes, peeled and cubed	2
1	small onion, chopped	1
5 cups	vegetable stock	1.25 L
2 cups	thawed frozen or canned corn kernels	500 mL
2 tbsp	Dijon mustard	30 mL
1/2 tsp	black pepper	2 mL
1/2 tsp	dried basil	2 mL
	or	
1 tbsp	chopped fresh basil	15 mL
1/2 tsp	sea salt	2 mL
1 cup	table cream	250 mL

1 In the pot, combine all of the ingredients, except the table cream, and bring the mixture to a boil on high heat. Immediately reduce the heat to medium and simmer the soup for about 15 minutes.

2 Using the hand blender, purée the soup until it is nice and smooth.

3 Add the cream and simmer the soup on medium heat for another 5 minutes. Serve.

The Best Western Sandwich with Herbs

Bone Rating:

Makes: 2 servings

Preparation Time:
 5 minutes

Cooking Time: 10 minutes

Cookware: Sauté pan,
 medium mixing bowl

> The western is also referred to as a Denver. Little Kenny wears a cowboy hat when he prepares this meal.

2 tbsp	butter	30 mL
2 tbsp	chopped celery	30 mL
2 tbsp	chopped green bell pepper	30 mL
2 tbsp	chopped green onion or chives	30 mL
2	large eggs, beaten	2
2 tbsp	chopped tomato	30 mL
1 tsp	chopped fresh parsley	5 mL
1/2 tsp	black pepper	2 mL
1/2 tsp	sea salt	2 mL
1/4 tsp	dried basil	1 mL
	or	
1/2 tsp	chopped fresh basil	2 mL
1/4 tsp	dried thyme	1 mL
	or	
1/2 tsp	chopped fresh thyme	2 mL
4	slices bread, toasted and buttered	4

> For a licorice flavor, replace the celery with chopped fennel. You'll love it.

1 In the sauté pan, melt the butter on medium heat until it starts to bubble. Add the celery, bell pepper and onion or chives and sauté for 2 to 3 minutes.

2 In the bowl, combine all the other ingredients, except the toast. Pour the egg mixture into the sauté pan and cook on medium heat for about 2 to 3 minutes, turning once to ensure that the eggs are done.

3 Split the egg mixture in half. Make two sandwiches with the toast and serve.

Little Kenny's mother helps him chop the celery, bell pepper, onion or chives, tomato and fresh parsley, basil and thyme.

To lower the fat content of this recipe, use margarine instead of butter.

Portobello Mushroom Pizza with Red Pepper

Bone Rating: 🦴

Makes: 2 servings

Preparation Time:
   10 minutes

Cooking Time: 15 minutes

Cookware: Baking sheet

Little Kenny's mother preheats the oven and helps him cut the stems off the mushroom caps, slice the onion, shred the cheese and chop the bell pepper and basil.

2	large portobello mushroom caps	2
1 tbsp	olive oil or spray	15 mL
1/2	small onion, thinly sliced	1/2
1/2 cup	shredded mozzarella cheese	125 mL
1/2 cup	finely chopped red bell pepper	125 mL
1/2 tsp	dried basil	2 mL
	or	
1 tbsp	finely chopped fresh basil	15 mL
1/2 tsp	black pepper	2 mL

1 Cut the stems off the mushrooms and clean the caps with a damp paper towel.

2 Brush or spray the mushroom caps with olive oil and place them on the baking sheet. Place half of the onion slices on top of each mushroom cap and sprinkle them evenly with the cheese. Add the red bell pepper, basil and black pepper.

3 Bake the mushroom caps in a preheated oven at 350°F (180°C) for 12 to 15 minutes, or until the cheese has melted.

41

Mother's Day Four-Cheese Rice and Broccoli

1	small red bell pepper, chopped	1
2 cups	broccoli florets	500 mL
2 cups	vegetable stock	500 mL
1 cup	long-grain white rice	250 mL
1/2 tsp	chili powder	2 mL
1/2 cup	sour cream	125 mL
1/4 cup	shredded Cheddar cheese	60 mL
1/4 cup	shredded Monterey Jack cheese	60 mL
1/4 cup	shredded mozzarella cheese	60 mL
2 tbsp	grated Parmesan cheese	30 mL

Bone Rating:

Makes: 4 to 6 servings

Preparation Time: 10 minutes

Cooking Time: 20 minutes

Cookware: Large pot

1 In the pot, combine all of the ingredients, except the sour cream and cheeses.

2 Bring the mixture to a boil on high heat, reduce the heat to medium and simmer the soup for about 15 minutes, or until the rice is cooked.

3 Add the sour cream and cheeses and mix well until the texture is creamy.

Little Kenny's mother helps him chop the bell pepper, cut the broccoli into florets and shred or grate the cheeses.

To lower the fat content of this recipe, use low-fat cheese and low-fat sour cream.

For a different taste and texture, replace any of the cheeses with Swiss, provolone, feta or goat cheese.

Rice, a cereal grain that originated in Asia, comes in over 1,000 varieties.

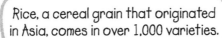

Mushroom Helper with Pasta and Cheese

Bone Rating:

Makes: 4 to 6 servings

Preparation Time:

   15 minutes

Cooking Time: 20 minutes

Cookware: Sauté pan or pot

> Cheddar cheese is the most popular cheese in the world. It originated in the village of Cheddar in Somerset, a region of England.

1/2 cup	vegetable stock	125 mL
2	cloves garlic, chopped	2
1	small onion, chopped	1
1	small red bell pepper, chopped	1
4 cups	chopped button mushrooms	1 L
2 cups	vegetable stock	500 mL
1 cup	macaroni	250 mL
1 cup	canned diced tomatoes	250 mL
1/2 tsp	dried basil	2 mL
	or	
1 tbsp	chopped fresh basil	15 mL
1/2 cup	shredded Cheddar cheese	125 mL
1/4 cup	table cream	60 mL

1 In the pan, heat the vegetable stock on medium heat and sauté the garlic, onion and red bell pepper for about 2 to 3 minutes.

2 Add all of the other ingredients, except the cheese and cream. Mix well and cook for 12 to 15 minutes on medium heat, stirring constantly.

3 Add the cheese and cream and continue to cook until the dish is nice and creamy, about 2 minutes.

Little Kenny's mother helps him chop the garlic, onion, bell pepper, mushrooms and basil and shred the cheese.

To lower the fat content of this recipe, use low-fat Cheddar cheese and skim milk instead of table cream.

Replace the vegetable stock with apple juice, which will give the dish a slightly sweet flavor.

Spaghetti Squash Curry

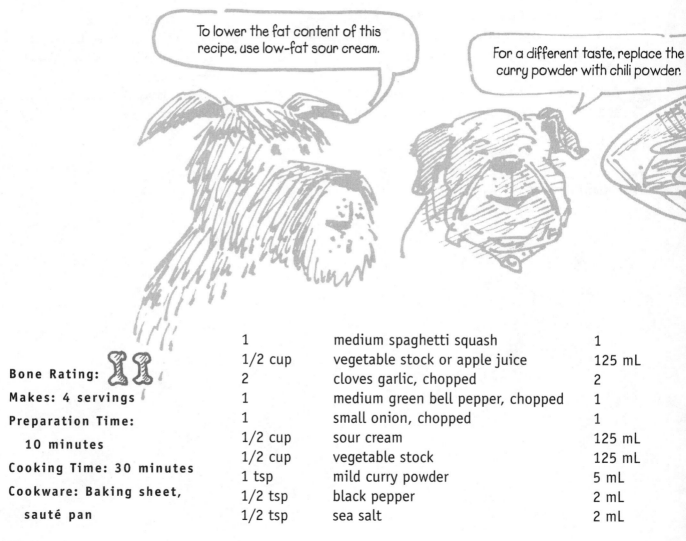

To lower the fat content of this recipe, use low-fat sour cream.

For a different taste, replace the curry powder with chili powder.

Bone Rating:

Makes: 4 servings

Preparation Time:
  10 minutes

Cooking Time: 30 minutes

Cookware: Baking sheet,
  sauté pan

1	medium spaghetti squash	1
1/2 cup	vegetable stock or apple juice	125 mL
2	cloves garlic, chopped	2
1	medium green bell pepper, chopped	1
1	small onion, chopped	1
1/2 cup	sour cream	125 mL
1/2 cup	vegetable stock	125 mL
1 tsp	mild curry powder	5 mL
1/2 tsp	black pepper	2 mL
1/2 tsp	sea salt	2 mL

Squash comes in two types, summer and winter squash. Spaghetti squash is a summer squash and is usually served with a sauce.

1. Place the squash on the baking sheet and bake in a pre-heated oven at 400°F (200°C) for 20 minutes.

2. In the sauté pan, heat the vegetable stock or apple juice over medium heat and sauté the garlic, green bell pepper and onion for about 3 to 4 minutes, or until tender. Add all of the other ingredients and cook for about 10 minutes, stirring occasionally.

3. Split the spaghetti squash and remove the seeds with a spoon. Remove the spaghetti-like insides of the squash with a fork and add it to the sauce. Mix well and serve.

Little Kenny's mother preheats the oven, splits the hot squash and removes the seeds and helps him chop the garlic, bell pepper and onion.

Green Stir-fry with Basil

Bone Rating:

Makes: 4 to 6 servings

Preparation Time:

   10 minutes

Cooking Time: 10 minutes

Cookware: Sauté pan

Replace the basil with oregano and the green onion with chives.

3/4 cup	vegetable stock	175 mL
2	medium green bell peppers, sliced	2
1	green apple, cored and slices	1
1	medium zucchini, sliced	1
2 cups	broccoli florets	500 mL
1 cup	trimmed and sliced snow peas	250 mL
1/2 tsp	dried basil	2 mL
	or	
1 tbsp	chopped fresh basil	15 mL
1/4 cup	soy sauce	60 mL
1/2 cup	chopped green onion	125 mL

❶ Heat the vegetable stock on high in the pan. Add all of the ingredients, except the soy sauce and green onion, and stir-fry on high for about 5 minutes, stirring constantly.

❷ Make a hole in the center of the stir-fry, add the soy sauce and reduce the heat to medium. Mix well and stir-fry for 2 minutes.

❸ Mix in the green onion and serve.

Little Kenny's mother helps him slice the green bell peppers, zucchini and snow peas, cut the broccoli into florets and chop the basil and green onion.

Spring Vegetables and Fusilli with Parmesan

Bone Rating:

Makes: 4 servings

Preparation Time:
  10 minutes

Cooking Time: 15 minutes

Cookware: Large pot

2	stalks celery, chopped	2
1	small onion, chopped	1
1	small red bell pepper, chopped	1
1	small zucchini, chopped	1
3 cups	vegetable stock	750 mL
2 cups	fusilli (spiral pasta), uncooked	500 mL
1 cup	canned diced tomatoes	250 mL
1/2 cup	grated carrot	125 mL
1/2 tsp	black pepper	2 mL
1/2 tsp	dried basil	2 mL
	or	
1 tbsp	chopped fresh basil	15 mL
1/2 tsp	dried thyme	2 mL
	or	
1 tbsp	chopped fresh thyme	15 mL
1/2 tsp	sea salt	2 mL
1/2 cup	grated Parmesan cheese	125 mL

Little Kenny loves this one-pot pasta. You can add or delete ingredients as you like.

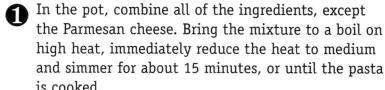

1 In the pot, combine all of the ingredients, except the Parmesan cheese. Bring the mixture to a boil on high heat, immediately reduce the heat to medium and simmer for about 15 minutes, or until the pasta is cooked.

2 Mix in the Parmesan cheese and serve.

Little Kenny's mother helps him chop the celery, onion, bell pepper, zucchini, fresh basil and fresh thyme and grate the cheese.

To lower the fat content of this recipe, use low-fat vegetable stock.

For a different taste and texture, replace the Parmesan cheese with shredded Cheddar cheese.

Little Kenny's Pad Thai

1 lb	fettuccine (egg noodles)	500 g
1/2 cup	vegetable stock	125 mL
1 lb	firm tofu, cut into cubes	500 g
2	cloves garlic, chopped	2
1	small onion, sliced	1
1	small red bell pepper, sliced	1
1 tbsp	chopped fresh ginger	15 mL
1/4 cup	ketchup	60 mL
1/4 cup	peanut butter	60 mL
1/4 cup	soy sauce	60 mL
1 tbsp	lemon juice	15 mL
1 tsp	sugar	5 mL
1/4 cup	chopped fresh coriander	60 mL
2 tbsp	unsalted crushed peanuts	30 mL

Bone Rating:

Makes: 4 servings

Preparation Time: 15 minutes

Cooking Time: 15 minutes

Cookware: Pot or sauté pan

Use apple juice instead of vegetable stock.

For a more traditional version, use rice noodles instead of egg noodles.

Pad Thai originated in Thailand. It usually includes peanuts and an assortment of other ingredients.

1 In the pot, cook the fettuccine in boiling water for about 7 to 8 minutes. Drain the pasta and set it aside.

2 Heat the vegetable stock in the sauté pan on high heat and sauté the tofu, garlic, onion, bell pepper and ginger for about 5 minutes, stirring constantly.

3 Add the remaining ingredients, except the coriander and peanuts, and stir-fry for 3 to 4 minutes. Add the pasta and toss for 2 minutes. Garnish with the coriander and peanuts.

Little Kenny's mother cooks and drains the pasta and helps him cube the tofu and chop the garlic, onion, bell pepper and fresh ginger and coriander.

Incredible Peanut Butter Cookies

Bone Rating: 🦴🦴🦴

Makes: 60 small cookies

Preparation Time:

10 minutes

Cooking Time: 15 minutes

Cookware: Medium mixing bowl, nonstick baking sheet

Little Kenny's mother preheats the oven.

1 1/4 cups	smooth peanut butter	310 mL
1 cup	butter, softened	250 mL
1 cup	brown sugar	250 mL
1 cup	granulated sugar	250 mL
2	large eggs	2
2 tsp	vanilla extract	10 mL
3 cups	flour	750 mL
2 tsp	baking soda	10 mL

1 In the bowl, blend the peanut butter and butter until the mixture is smooth. Add the brown and granulated sugar and mix well.

2 Add the eggs and vanilla and mix well. Blend in the flour and baking soda till the dough is soft.

3 Using a teaspoon, drop balls of the dough onto the baking sheet about 1 inch (2.5 cm) apart. Dip a fork in flour and press the back of the fork down lightly on the balls of dough in a criss-cross pattern. Bake the cookies in a preheated oven at 375°F (190°C) for 15 minutes, or until they are lightly browned.

Little Kenny and his friend Lorrie next door like to sit on the doorstep and eat these delicious cookies.

Little Kenny's Unbelievable Chocolate Chip Cookies

Bone Rating:

Makes: 60 cookies

Preparation Time:
   10 minutes

Cooking Time: 15 minutes

Cookware: Food processor
   or electric mixer,
   nonstick baking sheet

2 1/2 cups	brown sugar	625 mL
1 1/2 cups	shortening	375 mL
2	large eggs	2
1/4 cup	milk	60 mL
1 tbsp	vanilla extract	15 mL
3 cups	flour	750 mL
2 tsp	sea salt	10 mL
1 1/2 tsp	baking soda	7 mL
1/4 tsp	cinnamon	1 mL
3 cups	semisweet chocolate chips	750 mL

Little Kenny really enjoys making
these cookies at home with his
mom, Helen, and dad, Ed.

1. Using a food processor or electric mixer, blend the shortening and sugar on high for about 2 minutes. Add the eggs, milk and vanilla and blend on high for another 2 minutes.

2. Add the flour, salt, baking soda and cinnamon. Blend on low for 2 minutes and then, with the food processor still on low, gently stir in the chocolate chips.

3. Using a teaspoon, drop balls of dough onto the baking sheet about 1 1/2 inches (4 cm) apart. Bake the cookies in a preheated oven at 375°F (190°C) for 10 to 12 minutes.

Little Kenny's mother preheats the oven and helps him use the food processor or electric mixer.

Replace the chocolate chips with caramel or butterscotch chips.

Summer

Blueberry Muffins Extraordinaire / 60

Fabulous Carrot Pancakes / 62

Lazy Summer Salsa Scrambled Eggs with Parsley / 64

Fresh Fruit with Macaroni and Mint / 66

Grilled Vegetable Salad with Balsamic Vinegar / 68

Summer Potato Salad / 70

Chilled Pineapple Soup with Yogurt and Mint / 72

Chilled Strawberry Soup with Thyme / 74

Gazpacho with Fresh Herbs / 76

Focaccia Pizza with Olives and Feta / 78

Tomato and Basil Pizza with Goat Cheese on Phyllo / 80

Cheesy Vegetable Stew / 82

Greek Pasta with Spinach and Tomatoes / 84

Little Kenny's Simple Spaghetti and Tomato Sauce / 86

Mexican Beans and Rice with Coriander / 88

Mexican Stir-fry with Orange / 90

Original Stir-fry with Sesame Seeds / 92

Helen's Easy Strawberry Pie / 94

Long Weekend Apple-Peach Crisp / 96

Blueberry Muffins Extraordinaire

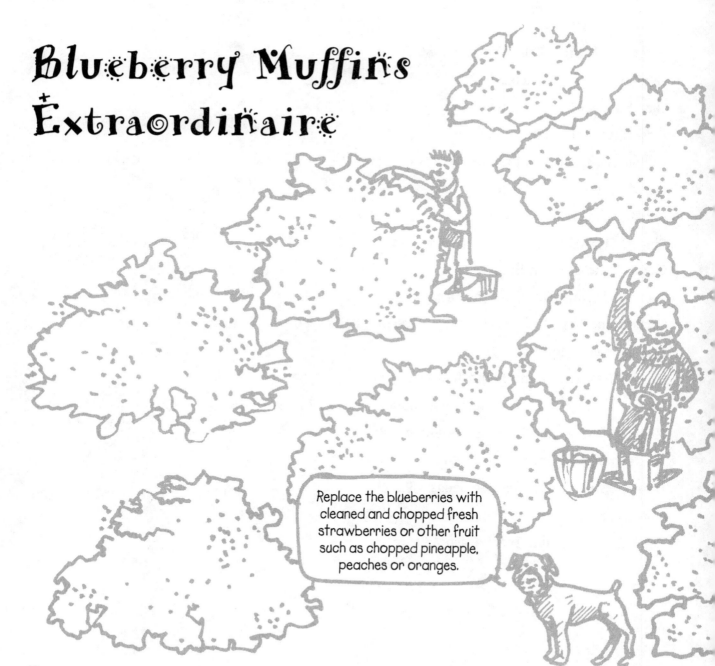

Replace the blueberries with cleaned and chopped fresh strawberries or other fruit such as chopped pineapple, peaches or oranges.

2 cups	flour	500 mL
1/4 cup	sugar	60 mL
2 tsp	baking powder	10 mL
1/2 tsp	sea salt	2 mL
2 cups	blueberries	500 mL
1	large egg, beaten	1
3/4 cup	milk	175 mL
1/4 cup	soft shortening	60 mL

Bone Rating:

Makes: 12 regular muffins or 24 mini muffins

Preparation Time: 10 minutes

Cooking Time: 20 minutes

Cookware: 2 medium mixing bowls, nonstick 12-muffin regular tin or 24-muffin mini-muffin tin

1 In one bowl, sift together the flour, sugar, baking powder and salt. Stir in the blueberries.

2 In the other bowl, combine the egg, milk and shortening. Add the dry mixture to the wet mixture and blend until they are just mixed. Be sure not to overmix the batter.

3 Spoon the batter into the muffin tins, filling each cup about two-thirds full. In an oven preheated to 400°F (200°C), bake regular muffins for about 20 minutes and mini muffins for about 15 minutes, or until the muffins are browned.

Little Kenny's mother preheats the oven.

Little Kenny serves these blueberry muffins for breakfast or dessert.

To lower the fat content of this recipe, use low-fat or skim milk instead of regular milk.

Fabulous Carrot Pancakes

To lower the fat content of this recipe, use skim milk.

Little Kenny's mother helps him grate the carrots and onion and chop the fresh basil.

Bone Rating: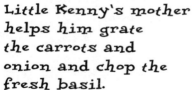

Makes: 4 servings

Preparation Time:
  15 minutes

Cooking Time: 15 minutes

Cookware: Food processor, large mixing bowl, nonstick sauté pan

4	medium carrots	4
1/2	small onion	1/2
2	large eggs	2
1 cup	flour	250 mL
1 cup	milk	250 mL
1 tsp	baking powder	5 mL
1/2 tsp	black pepper	2 mL
1/2 tsp	dried basil	2 mL
	or	
1 tbsp	chopped fresh basil	15 mL
1/2 tsp	sea salt	2 mL
1/4 tsp	cinnamon	1 mL

1. Grate the carrots and onion in a food processor.

2. Place all of the ingredients in the bowl and mix well.

3. Heat the pan over medium heat. Ladle small amounts of the mixture into the pan and cook for about 2 to 3 minutes on each side, or until golden brown.

63

Lazy Summer Salsa Scrambled Eggs with Parsley

Bone Rating: 🦴

Makes: 4 servings

Preparation Time:
   10 minutes

Cooking Time: 10 minutes

Cookware: Mixing bowl,
   sauté pan

6	medium eggs	6
1/2 cup	chopped green onion	125 mL
1/2 cup	mild salsa	125 mL
1/4 cup	chopped fresh parsley	60 mL
1/4 cup	milk	60 mL
1 tbsp	butter	15 mL

To lower the fat content of this recipe, use skim or nonfat milk instead of regular milk, and margarine instead of butter.

Little Kenny likes to prepare this quick and easy but flavorful breakfast for his parents on weekends.

1. In the bowl, combine all of the ingredients, except the butter, and whisk together.

2. In the sauté pan, melt the butter over medium heat until it starts to bubble. Pour in egg mixture and cook, stirring constantly, for about 5 minutes, or until the eggs are done.

Little Kenny's mother helps him chop the green onion and fresh parsley.

Replace the fresh parsley with fresh coriander.

Fresh Fruit with Macaroni and Mint

Bone Rating:

Makes: 4 servings

Preparation Time:
   10 minutes

Cookware: Large mixing
   bowl

Little Kenny's mother cooks and drains the pasta and helps him chop the apple, orange, pear, pineapple and fresh mint.

2 cups	cooked macaroni, cooled	500 mL
1	medium apple, peeled, cored and chopped	1
1	medium orange, peeled, seeded and chopped	1
1	medium pear, peeled, cored and chopped	1
1 cup	chopped pineapple	250 mL
1 cup	plain yogurt	250 mL
1/2 cup	liquid honey	125 mL
2 tbsp	chopped fresh mint	30 mL

❶ In the bowl, combine the macaroni with the fruit. Toss well.

❷ Add the yogurt, honey and mint and mix well.

❸ Refrigerate the fruit salad for at least 30 minutes before serving.

Grilled Vegetable Salad with Balsamic Vinegar

Little Kenny often makes this salad in advance and serves it cold.

Add other vegetables such as thinly sliced carrot, eggplant or even fennel.

Bone Rating: 🦴🦴
Makes: 4 to 6 servings
Preparation Time:
  10 minutes
Cooking Time: 10 minutes
Cookware: Grill or grill pan

8	spears asparagus, blanched	8
2	medium portobello mushroom caps	2
2	medium zucchini, sliced into 4 lengthwise	2
1	medium onion, cut into 1/2-inch (1 cm) slices	1
	Olive oil or vegetable spray	
3 cups	mixed salad greens (mesclun)	750 mL
1/4 cup	balsamic vinegar	60 mL
1/4 cup	chopped fresh parsley	60 mL

Little Kenny's mother blanches the asparagus and grills the vegetables, and helps him slice the zucchini, onion and grilled portobello mushrooms and chop the fresh parsley.

To "blanch" vegetables means to put them in boiling water for 2 to 3 minutes so that they are partially cooked. Usually you remove the vegetables from the boiling water right away and rinse them in cold water or ice water to stop them from cooking more.

1 Spray the mushroom caps and zucchini and onion slices lightly with the olive oil or vegetable spray.

2 Grill the mushroom caps and zucchini and onion slices on a hot grill or grill pan, turning them once to get grill marks. (If you don't have a grill or grill pan, place the vegetables on a baking sheet and grill them under the broiler.)

3 Place the mixed salad greens on a serving platter. Slice the portobello mushroom caps and place them on the greens. Top with the other vegetables and drizzle with the balsamic vinegar. Sprinkle with fresh parsley and serve.

Summer Potato Salad

Bone Rating: 🦴🦴
Makes: 4 to 6 servings
Preparation Time:
   10 minutes
Cooking Time: 15 minutes
Cookware: Pot, large
   mixing bowl

4	medium potatoes, peeled and cut into bite-sized pieces	4
2	hard-cooked large eggs, thinly sliced	2
2	stalks celery, finely chopped	2
1/4 cup	finely chopped green onion or chives	60 mL
1/2 cup	mayonnaise	125 mL
2 tbsp	olive oil	30 mL
1/2 tsp	black pepper	2 mL
1/2 tsp	sea salt	2 mL
1/4 cup	chopped fresh parsley	60 mL

Little Kenny always makes this simple yet flavorful spud salad in the summer because it is perfect for picnics and barbecues.

To lower the fat content of this recipe, use low-fat mayonnaise.

1. Cook the potatoes in a pot of boiling water over medium heat for about 15 minutes, or until tender. Drain and allow to cool.

2. In the bowl, combine the potatoes, eggs, celery and greens onions. Mix gently.

3. Add the mayonnaise, olive oil, black pepper and salt. Mix gently. Refrigerate the salad for at least 30 minutes. Garnish with the fresh parsley and serve.

Little Kenny's mother helps him peel, cut, boil and drain the potatoes, boil and slice the eggs and chop the celery, green onions and fresh parsley.

To give this salad a licorice flavor, replace the celery with 1/2 cup (125 mL) finely chopped fennel.

Chilled Pineapple Soup with Yogurt and Mint

There are over 30 different types of mint, but the most common are peppermint and spearmint.

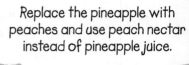

Replace the pineapple with peaches and use peach nectar instead of pineapple juice.

Bone Rating:

Makes: 4 to 6 servings

Preparation Time:
  15 minutes

Cookware: Large mixing
  bowl or pot

4 cups	pineapple juice	1 L
3 cups	chopped pineapple, fresh or canned	750 mL
1 cup	plain yogurt	250 mL
1/2 cup	apple juice	125 mL
2 tbsp	liquid honey	30 mL
1/2 tsp	dried mint	2 mL
	or	
1 tbsp	chopped fresh mint	15 mL
1/4 tsp	cinnamon	1 mL

To lower the fat content of this recipe, use low-fat or nonfat yogurt.

1 In the bowl or pot, combine all of the ingredients and mix well.

2 Refrigerate the soup for at least 1 hour before serving.

Little Kenny's mother helps him chop the pineapple and fresh mint.

Chilled Strawberry Soup with Thyme

Bone Rating:

Makes: 4 to 6 servings

Preparation Time:
   15 minutes

Cookware: Large mixing bowl or pot

3 1/2 cups	washed chopped fresh strawberries	875 mL
3 1/2 cups	cranberry juice	875 mL
1 cup	plain yogurt	250 mL
1/2 cup	apple juice	125 mL
1/2 cup	table cream	125 mL
2 tbsp	liquid honey	30 mL
1/2 tsp	dried thyme	2 mL
	or	
1 tbsp	chopped fresh thyme	15 mL

1 In the bowl or pot, combine all of the ingredients and mix well.

2 Refrigerate the soup for at least 1 hour before serving.

Little Kenny's mother helps him chop the strawberries and fresh thyme.

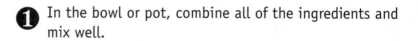

The strawberry is a distant relative of the rose and has grown wild for hundreds of years in both the Americas and Europe.

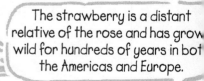

Gazpacho with Fresh Herbs

2	stalks celery, finely chopped	2	
1	small cucumber, diced	1	
1	small green bell pepper, finely chopped	1	
1	small red bell pepper, finely chopped	1	
1	small onion, finely chopped	1	
1	can (28 oz/796 mL) diced tomatoes	1	
4 cups	vegetable stock	1 L	
1 cup	tomato juice	250 mL	
2 tbsp	chopped fresh basil	30 mL	
2 tbsp	chopped fresh dill	30 mL	
2 tbsp	chopped fresh parsley	30 mL	
1 tsp	chili powder	5 mL	
1/2 tsp	black pepper	2 mL	
1/2 tsp	sea salt	2 mL	

Bone Rating: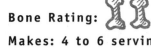

Makes: 4 to 6 servings

Preparation Time:

15 minutes

Cookware: Large mixing bowl or pot

Little Kenny's mother helps him chop the celery, bell peppers, onion, basil, dill and parsley and dice the cucumber.

❶ Combine all of the ingredients in the bowl or pot. Mix well.

❷ Refrigerate the soup for at least 1 hour before serving, allowing the flavors to mingle. Serve with a nice mixed salad.

Add any other vegetables you like to gazpacho, keeping in mind that some may need to be cooked first.

Little Kenny sometimes heats up 2 cups (500 mL) of this soup to serve as a pasta sauce.

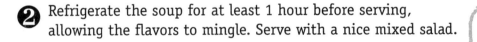

Focaccia Pizza with Olives and Feta

1	small focaccia bread, plain or flavored	1
1 tbsp	olive oil	15 mL
3/4 cup	crumbled feta cheese	175 mL
1/2 cup	chopped olives	125 mL
1/2 tsp	dried rosemary	2 mL
	or	
1 tbsp	fresh rosemary	15 mL

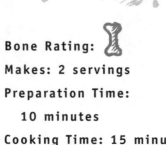

Little Kenny loves to use focaccia bread as a pizza crust for those days he wants a fuller meal.

Bone Rating:

Makes: 2 servings

Preparation Time:
  10 minutes

Cooking Time: 15 minutes

Cookware: Baking sheet

1. Place the focaccia bread on the baking sheet and evenly brush the olive oil over the bread.

2. Distribute the feta cheese and olives on the bread. Sprinkle the rosemary on top.

3. Bake the pizza in a preheated oven at 375°F (190°C) for 15 minutes. Allow to cool for a few minutes before cutting and serving.

Little Kenny's mother helps him preheat the oven and chop the olives and fresh rosemary.

To lower the fat content of this recipe use light or low-fat feta cheese.

Replace the olives with 3/4 cup (175 mL) chopped sun-dried tomatoes.

Tomato and Basil Pizza with Goat Cheese on Phyllo

Bone Rating: 🦴🦴

Makes: 4 to 6 servings

Preparation Time:
   10 minutes

Cooking Time: 15 minutes

Cookware: Small mixing
   bowl, baking sheet

1/4 cup	olive oil	60 mL
1/4 cup	melted butter	60 mL
1/2 tsp	garlic or onion powder	2 mL
7	phyllo sheets	7
2	ripe tomatoes, thinly sliced	2
3/4 cup	crumbled goat cheese	175 mL
1 tsp	dried basil	5 mL
	or	
1 tbsp	chopped fresh basil	15 mL
1/2 tsp	black pepper	2 mL

This is a great dish to serve warm or cold at a party or to take on a summer picnic and serve with a salad.

Replace the goat cheese with feta, Cheddar or mozzarella cheese.

1. In the bowl, combine the olive oil, butter and garlic or onion powder. Brush the mixture over each phyllo sheet and stack them on the baking sheet.

2. Distribute the tomatoes, goat cheese, basil and black pepper evenly on top of the phyllo.

3. Bake the pizza in a preheated oven at 400°F (200°C) for 15 minutes, or until the phyllo is brown and the cheese has softened.

Little Kenny's mother preheats the oven and helps him melt the butter, slice the tomatoes and chop the fresh basil.

To lower the fat content of this recipe, use margarine instead of butter.

1	can (28 oz/796 mL) diced tomatoes	1
2	cloves garlic, chopped	2
2	medium carrots, chopped	2
2	stalks celery, chopped	2
1	small onion, chopped	1
1	small potato, peeled and cut into small cubes	1
1	small zucchini, chopped	1
3 cups	vegetable stock	750 mL
1 cup	broccoli florets	250 mL
1/2 tsp	black pepper	2 mL
1/2 tsp	dried basil	2 mL
	or	
1 tbsp	chopped fresh basil	15 mL
1/2 tsp	sea salt	2 mL
1/2 cup	shredded Cheddar cheese	125 mL
1/2 cup	shredded mozzarella cheese	125 mL

Bone Rating:

Makes: 4 to 6 servings

Preparation Time:
   10 minutes

Cooking Time: 20 minutes

Cookware: Large pot

Little Kenny's mother helps him chop the garlic, carrots, celery, onion, zucchini and fresh basil, cut the potato into cubes and the broccoli into florets and shred the cheeses.

❶ In the pot, combine all of the ingredients, except the cheeses, and bring to a boil over high heat. Reduce the heat to medium and simmer the mixture for about 15 minutes.

❷ Add the cheeses and mix well, allowing the cheese to melt.

❸ Serve right away.

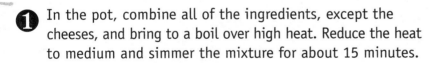

This stew is a great way to use up all of the vegetables in your refrigerator.

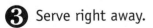

Greek Pasta with Spinach and Tomatoes

Spinach is not only healthy, but also very flavorful in dishes like salads, pasta, quiche, soups and stews.

Replace the black olives with green olives or with 1/2 cup (125 mL) chopped sun-dried tomatoes.

Bone Rating:

Makes: 4 to 6

Preparation Time:
   10 minutes

Cooking Time: 15 minutes

Cookware: Large pot,
   sauté pan

2 cups	rotini (spiral pasta)	500 mL
1/2 cup	vegetable stock	125 mL
1	clove garlic, chopped	1
1	small onion, chopped	1
2	medium tomatoes, chopped	2
2 cups	chopped spinach	500 mL
1/2 cup	black olives	125 mL
1/2 cup	tomato juice	125 mL
1/2 tsp	dried oregano	2 mL
	or	
1 tbsp	chopped fresh oregano	15 mL
1/2 tsp	black pepper	2 mL
1/2 tsp	sea salt	2 mL

To lower the fat content of this recipe, use low-fat vegetable stock.

1 In the pot, cook the rotini in boiling water for about 7 to 8 minutes. Drain the pasta and set it aside.

2 In the sauté pan, heat the vegetable stock over medium heat and gently sauté the garlic and onion for about 3 to 4 minutes. Add all of the other ingredients and simmer the sauce on low heat for about 5 minutes.

3 Add the pasta to the sauté pan and mix it well with the sauce before serving.

Little Kenny's mother cooks and drains the pasta and helps him chop the garlic, onion, tomatoes, spinach and fresh oregano.

Little Kenny's Simple Spaghetti and Tomato Sauce

Bone Rating:

Makes: 4 to 6 servings

Preparation Time:
   10 minutes

Cooking Time: 15 minutes

Cookware: Large pot,
   large sauté pan

1 lb	spaghetti	500 g
1/2 cup	vegetable stock	125 mL
2	cloves garlic, chopped	2
1	small onion, chopped	1
1 cup	canned diced tomatoes	250 mL
1/2 cup	mild salsa	125 mL
1/2 tsp	black pepper	2 mL
1/2 tsp	dried basil	2 mL
	or	
1 tbsp	chopped fresh basil	15 mL
1/2 tsp	sea salt	2 mL
1/4 cup	chopped fresh parsley	60 mL
1/4 cup	grated Parmesan cheese	60 mL

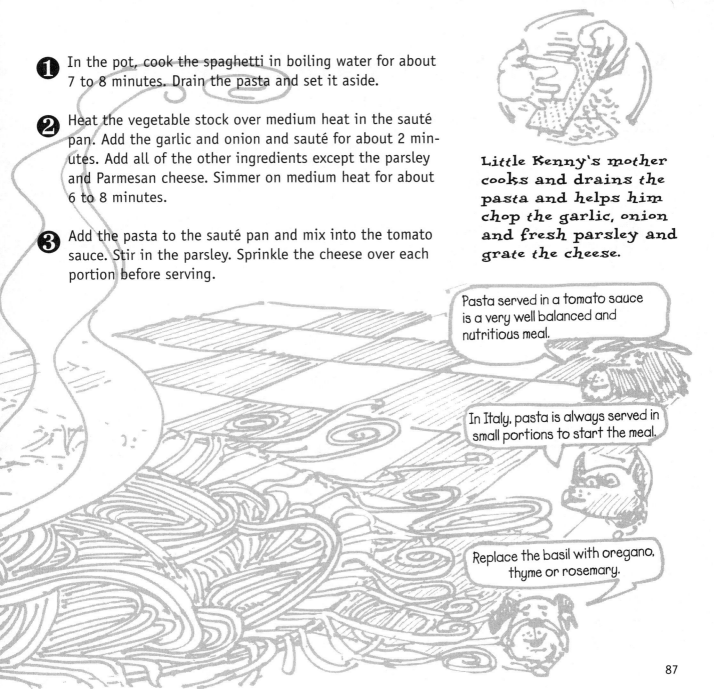

1. In the pot, cook the spaghetti in boiling water for about 7 to 8 minutes. Drain the pasta and set it aside.

2. Heat the vegetable stock over medium heat in the sauté pan. Add the garlic and onion and sauté for about 2 minutes. Add all of the other ingredients except the parsley and Parmesan cheese. Simmer on medium heat for about 6 to 8 minutes.

3. Add the pasta to the sauté pan and mix into the tomato sauce. Stir in the parsley. Sprinkle the cheese over each portion before serving.

Little Kenny's mother cooks and drains the pasta and helps him chop the garlic, onion and fresh parsley and grate the cheese.

Pasta served in a tomato sauce is a very well balanced and nutritious meal.

In Italy, pasta is always served in small portions to start the meal.

Replace the basil with oregano, thyme or rosemary.

Mexican Beans and Rice with Coriander

Combining the rice, which is a carbohydrate, and the beans, which are a good source of protein, produces a well-balanced meal.

Rice and beans are a staple in most Latin American countries, where people eat them at almost every meal.

Replace the kidney bean with white, navy or blac beans. This dish is really tasty with lentils, too.

Bone Rating:

Makes: 4 to 6 servings

Preparation Time:

   10 minutes

Cooking Time: 20 minutes

Cookware: Large sauté pan

1/2 cup	apple juice	125 mL	
1	clove garlic, chopped	1	
1	small green bell pepper, chopped	1	
1	small onion, chopped	1	
2 cups	vegetable broth	500 mL	
1 cup	long-grain white rice	250 mL	
1 cup	drained canned red kidney beans	250 mL	
1 cup	canned diced tomatoes	250 mL	
1/2 cup	frozen or canned corn kernels	125 mL	
1/2 tsp	chili powder	2 mL	
1/4 cup	chopped fresh coriander	60 mL	

1. In the sauté pan, heat the apple juice over medium heat and sauté the garlic, bell pepper and onion for about 2 minutes.

2. Add all of the other ingredients except the coriander. Bring to a boil on high heat. Cover, reduce the heat to medium and simmer for about 20 minutes, or until the rice is tender.

3. Stir in the fresh coriander before serving.

Little Kenny's mother helps him chop the garlic, bell pepper, onion and fresh coriander.

Mexican Stir-fry with Orange

Little Kenny's mother helps him cut the carrot, bell peppers, zucchini and orange, slice the onion and chop the fresh coriander.

Replace the orange and orange juice with grapefruit and grapefruit juice.

3/4 cup	orange juice	175 mL
1	large carrot, cut thinly on the diagonal	1
1	medium green bell pepper, cut into strips	1
1	medium sweet red bell pepper, cut into strips	1
1	medium zucchini, cut into 1/4-inch (.5 cm) strips	1
1	small onion, sliced	1
1	small orange, peeled, seeded and cut into pieces	1
1/2 tsp	chili powder	2 mL
1/4 cup	orange juice	60 mL
1/4 cup	chopped fresh coriander	60 mL

Bone Rating:

Makes: 4 servings

Preparation Time:
10 minutes

Cooking Time: 15 minutes

Cookware: Sauté pan

1 Heat the orange juice in the sauté pan on high heat and stir-fry the carrot, bell peppers, zucchini and onion for about 8 minutes.

2 Add the orange and chili powder and stir-fry for another 2 to 3 minutes.

3 Add the orange juice to the center of the pan and gently mix the vegetables around. Sprinkle the coriander on top of the stir-fry before serving.

Oranges, which originated in China, come in several varieties, such as blood, clementine, Mandarin, navel and Valencia.

Oranges are packed with vitamin C and are great alone or in salads, baking, drinks or—as in this dish—a stir-fry.

91

Original Stir-fry with Sesame Seeds

To lower the salt content of this recipe, use low-sodium soy sauce.

I would add 1/2 cup (125 mL) bean sprouts or even 1/2 cup (125 mL) sliced water chestnuts.

Little Kenny's mother helps him chop the garlic and fresh coriander, slice the onion, bell pepper, snow peas and green onions and cut the broccoli into florets.

Bone Rating: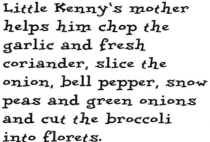

Makes: 4 servings

Preparation Time:
10 minutes

Cooking Time: 15 minutes

Cookware: Sauté pan

3/4 cup	vegetable stock	175 mL
2	cloves garlic, chopped	2
1	small onion, sliced	1
1	small red bell pepper, thinly sliced	1
1 cup	broccoli florets	250 mL
1 cup	trimmed and thinly sliced snow peas	250 mL
1/4 cup	soy sauce	60 mL
2	green onions, sliced lengthwise	2
1/4 cup	chopped fresh coriander	60 mL
2 tbsp	sesame seeds	30 mL

For extra flavor, add 1 tsp (5 mL) sesame oil to the vegetable stock.

1 Heat the vegetable stock in the sauté pan on high heat and gently stir-fry the garlic, onion, bell pepper, broccoli and snow peas for about 5 minutes.

2 Add the soy sauce to the center of the mixture, reduce the heat to medium and stir-fry for about 2 to 3 minutes.

3 Add the green onions and stir-fry for 2 minutes. Sprinkle the coriander and sesame seeds on top of the stir-fry before serving.

Helen's Easy Strawberry Pie

Bone Rating:

Makes: 6 servings

Preparation Time:

15 minutes

Cooking Time: 30 minutes

Cookware: Medium mixing bowl

4 cups	washed and halved fresh strawberries	1 L
1 cup	sugar	250 mL
1/3 cup	flour	80 mL
1/2 tsp	cinnamon	2 mL
2	9-inch (23 cm) frozen pie shells, one in pan, other for top	2
1/4 cup	butter, softened	60 mL

① In the bowl, combine the strawberries, sugar, flour and cinnamon. Gently mix together.

② Place the strawberry mixture in the pie shell in the pan and cover with the other pie shell. Seal the edges by pressing them together with your fingers. Make a slit in the center of the top crust and brush the butter on top.

③ Bake the pie in a preheated oven at 375°F (190°C) for about 30 minutes.

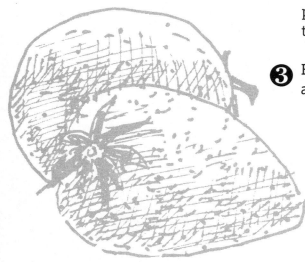

Long Weekend Apple-Peach Crisp

Bone Rating: 🦴🦴

Makes: 4 servings

Preparation Time: 15 minutes

Cooking Time: 20 to 25 minutes

Cookware: 2 medium mixing bowls, nonstick 9-inch (23-cm) pie plate

4	small apples, peeled, cored and chopped	4
3	medium peaches, pitted and chopped	3
3 tbsp	granulated sugar	45 mL
1/2 cup	rolled oats	125 mL
1/4 cup	brown sugar	60 mL
2 tbsp	flour	30 mL
1/2 tsp	cinnamon	2 mL
2 tbsp	butter, softened	30 mL

To lower the fat content of this recipe, use margarine instead of butter.

Replace the apples with pears when they are in season.

1. In one bowl, combine the apples, peaches and granulated sugar. Mix well.

2. In the other bowl, combine the oats, brown sugar, flour and cinnamon. Gently add the butter and mix.

3. Place the apple mixture in the pie plate and top with the oat mixture. Bake the crisp in a preheated oven at 375°F (190°C) for 20 to 25 minutes, or until the topping is golden and the apple is soft when tested with a fork.

Little Kenny's mother preheats the oven and helps him peel, core and chop the apples and pit and chop the peaches.

The peach is actually a distant relative of the rose and is used in a variety of ways in desserts, fish and meat dishes, jams and preserves.

Fall

Little Kenny's Bran Muffins Fantastic / 100

Scrambled Eggs with Onion, Parmesan and Red Pepper / 102

Sleepy Kenny's Wakeup Breakfast Soup / 104

Couscous Salad with Raisins and Parsley Madness / 106

Little Kenny's Mighty Caesar Salad / 108

Little Kenny's Mashed Potato Soup with Cheddar Cheese / 110

Spooky Halloween Pumpkin Soup with Apple / 112

Fabulous Mushroom and Pineapple Pita Pizza / 114

Potato and Onion Pizza / 116

Fall Bell Pepper Sauté / 118

Mexican Fried Rice Little Kenny Style / 120

Penne with Garlic and Fresh Herbs / 122

Rotini with Chickpeas and Tomatoes / 124

Thanksgiving Portobello Stir-Fry / 126

Tofu Lo Mein / 128

Fall Apple Crisp / 130

Maple Syrup Bread Pudding / 132

Little Kenny's Bran Muffins Fantastic

4 cups	bran cereal	1 L	
1 1/2 cups	sugar	375 mL	
1 1/2 cups	raisins	375 mL	
3/4 cup	vegetable oil	175 mL	
3/4 cup	warm water	175 mL	
3	large eggs	3	
1/2 cup	milk	125 mL	
3 cups	flour	750 mL	
1/2 tsp	baking soda	2 mL	
1/4 tsp	sea salt	1 mL	

Bone Rating:

Makes: 24 regular muffins or 48 mini muffins

Preparation Time: 10 minutes

Cooking Time: 30 minutes

Cookware: Large mixing bowl, nonstick 12-muffin regular tin or 24-muffin mini-muffin tin

1 In the bowl, combine the bran cereal, sugar, raisins, oil, water, eggs and milk. Mix well.

2 Add the flour, baking soda and salt and continue to mix until the wet and dry ingredients are combined.

3 Spoon the batter into the muffin tins, filling each cup about half full. Bake the muffins in a preheated oven at 350°F (180°C) for 30 minutes, or until browned.

Little Kenny's mother preheats the oven.

Little Kenny's mother, Helen, used to make these muffins for Kenny's grandfather many years ago.

Scrambled Eggs with Onion, Parmesan and Red Pepper

Bone Rating:

Makes: 4 servings

Preparation Time: 5 minutes

Cooking Time: 5 to 8 minutes

Cookware: Large mixing bowl, large sauté pan

2	large green onions, finely chopped	2
1	small red bell pepper, finely chopped	1
1/4 cup	milk	60 mL
4	large eggs	4
1/4 cup	finely chopped fresh parsley	60 mL
2 tbsp	grated Parmesan cheese	30 mL
1/2 tsp	black pepper	2 mL
1/2 tsp	sea salt	2 mL
2 tbsp	butter	30 mL
4	English muffins	4

Little Kenny's mother helps him chop the green onions, bell pepper and parsley and grate the cheese.

To lower the fat content of this recipe, use skim milk.

Waking up in the morning to the aroma of eggs and toast is very delightful.

Replace the Parmesan cheese with mozzarella, Cheddar or feta cheese. Delicious!

1 In the bowl, whisk together the green onions, bell pepper, milk, eggs, parsley, cheese, pepper and salt.

2 In the sauté pan, melt the butter over medium heat until it starts to bubble. Add the egg mixture and cook until it is firm.

3 Split the English muffins in half. Distribute the scrambled eggs evenly on top of each English muffin half and serve.

Sleepy Kenny's Wakeup Breakfast Soup

Bone Rating:

Makes: 4 servings

Preparation Time:
    10 minutes

Cooking Time: 15 minutes

Cookware: Medium pot,
    small mixing bowl

5 cups	vegetable stock	1.25 L
1	small onion, chopped	1
1	small red bell pepper, chopped	1
1/2 tsp	black pepper	2 mL
5	medium eggs	5
1/2 cup	shredded Cheddar cheese	125 mL
1 cup	croutons	250 mL

Little Kenny calls this his breakfast soup because it has eggs and toast, which are a great start to the day.

To lower the fat content of this recipe, use low-fat Cheddar cheese.

1. Place the vegetable stock, onion, bell pepper and black pepper in the pot. Bring the mixture to a boil over high heat, reduce the heat to medium and simmer the soup for about 5 minutes.

2. In the bowl, whisk the eggs until smooth. Pour the eggs into the soup and continue mixing for 3 to 4 minutes to prevent the eggs from sticking together.

3. Add the cheese and stir for 1 minute. Add the croutons and serve.

Little Kenny's mother helps him chop the onion and red bell pepper and shred the cheese.

You can use many other cheeses in this soup. The most popular cheeses are Parmesan, Swiss and mozzarella. Little Kenny's favorite is Cheddar cheese. What is yours?

105

Couscous Salad with Raisins and Parsley Madness

Granular semolina, also called couscous, is a staple of the North African diet. Little Kenny loves to use it because it is so versatile and quick to prepare.

Couscous is a good source of protein and carbohydrates.

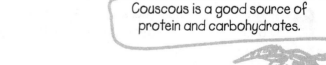

Bone Rating:

Makes: 4 servings

Preparation Time:
   10 minutes

Cookware: Small pot,
   medium and small
   mixing bowls

2 cups	apple juice or water	250 mL
1 1/2 cups	couscous	375 mL
3/4 cup	raisins	175 mL
1 cup	canned chickpeas, rinsed and drained	250 mL
1/2 cup	chopped green onion	125 mL
1/2 cup	canned diced tomatoes, drained	125 mL
1/3 cup	apple cider vinegar	80 mL
1/4 cup	olive oil	60 mL
1/2 tsp	black pepper	2 mL
1/2 tsp	dried basil	2 mL
	or	
1 tbsp	chopped fresh basil	15 mL
1/2 tsp	sea salt	2 mL
3/4 cup	finely chopped parsley	175 mL

Little Kenny's mother helps him boil the apple juice or water and chop the green onions, basil and parsley.

Not everyone loves raisins as much as Little Kenny does. You can replace them with peeled and chopped apple or pear.

1 Bring the apple juice or water to a boil in the pot. Place the couscous and raisins in the medium bowl with the boiling apple juice or water. Cover, and let the mixture stand for about 10 minutes, occasionally fluffing the couscous with a fork.

2 Add the chickpeas, green onions and tomatoes and mix well.

3 In the small bowl, whisk together the vinegar, olive oil, black pepper, basil and salt. Add this mixture and the parsley to the couscous, stir and serve.

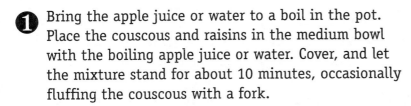

Little Kenny's Mighty Caesar Salad

Bone Rating:

Makes: 4 servings

Preparation Time:
   10 minutes

Cookware: Small and large
   mixing bowls

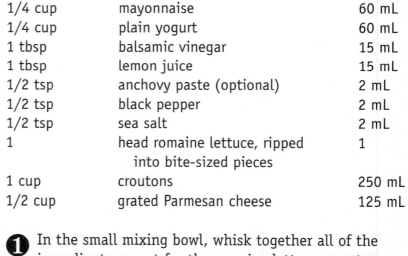

Little Kenny's mother helps him chop the garlic.

To lower the fat content of this recipe, use low-fat yogurt and low-fat mayonnaise.

3	cloves garlic, chopped	3
1/4 cup	mayonnaise	60 mL
1/4 cup	plain yogurt	60 mL
1 tbsp	balsamic vinegar	15 mL
1 tbsp	lemon juice	15 mL
1/2 tsp	anchovy paste (optional)	2 mL
1/2 tsp	black pepper	2 mL
1/2 tsp	sea salt	2 mL
1	head romaine lettuce, ripped into bite-sized pieces	1
1 cup	croutons	250 mL
1/2 cup	grated Parmesan cheese	125 mL

1 In the small mixing bowl, whisk together all of the ingredients except for the romaine lettuce, croutons and Parmesan cheese. Blend until smooth.

2 Place the romaine lettuce in the large bowl and toss with the dressing just before serving. Add the Parmesan cheese and croutons and serve.

Little Kenny prefers to have only the heart, or center, of the lettuce in his salad. Try it and see whether you prefer it or the greener leaves.

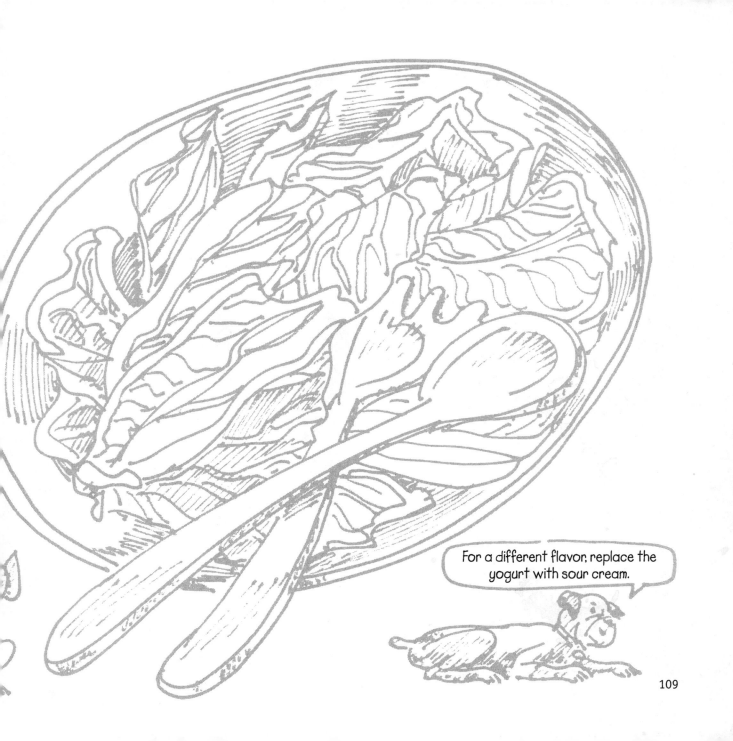

For a different flavor, replace the yogurt with sour cream.

Little Kenny's Mashed Potato Soup with Cheddar Cheese

Little Kenny's mother helps him peel and cube the potatoes, chop the garlic, onion, red bell pepper and basil and shred the cheese.

To lower the fat content of this recipe, use skim milk instead of table cream (or use neither) and low-fat Cheddar cheese.

4	large potatoes, peeled and cubed	4
2	cloves garlic, chopped	2
1	small onion, chopped	1
1	small red bell pepper, chopped	1
4 cups	vegetable stock	1 L
1/2 tsp	black pepper	2 mL
1/2 tsp	chili powder	2 mL
1/2 tsp	dried basil	2 mL
	or	
1 tbsp	chopped fresh basil	15 mL
1/2 tsp	sea salt	2 mL
3/4 cup	shredded Cheddar cheese	175 mL
1/2 cup	table cream	125 mL

Bone Rating: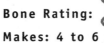

Makes: 4 to 6 servings

Preparation Time:

10 minutes

Cooking Time: 20 minutes

Cookware: Medium pot,

hand blender

1 In the pot, mix all of the ingredients except the cheese and cream. Bring the mixture to a boil, reduce the heat to medium and simmer for about 15 minutes, or until the potatoes are cooked.

2 Using the hand blender, purée the soup until smooth.

3 Gently mix the cheese and the cream into the soup and simmer over low heat for 2 to 3 minutes. Serve warm.

This is a perfect recipe for using up leftover Thanksgiving mashed potatoes. Use 3 cups (750 mL) in this recipe. Yum yum.

The potato is a member of the same family as the tomato and eggplant.

Spooky Halloween Pumpkin Soup with Apple

Bone Rating:

Makes: 4 to 6 servings

Preparation Time:
   10 minutes

Cooking Time: 20 minutes

Cookware: Medium pot

1 tbsp	butter	15 mL
1	large apple, peeled, cored and cut into small cubes	1
1	small onion, chopped	1
1 cup	apple juice	250 mL
5 cups	vegetable stock	1.25 L
1 cup	puréed cooked pumpkin or canned pumpkin	250 mL
1/2 cup	apple sauce	125 mL
1 tbsp	brown sugar	15 mL
1/2 tsp	dried thyme	2 mL
	or	
1 tbsp	chopped fresh thyme	15 mL
1/2 tsp	sea salt	2 mL
1/4 tsp	cinnamon	1 mL
1/2 cup	table cream (optional)	125 mL

To lower the fat content of this recipe, use one-quarter table cream and three-quarters skim milk.

You can replace the apple with pear and use pear nectar instead of apple juice

1 In the pot, melt the butter over medium heat until it begins to bubble. Add the apple and onion and sauté for 3 to 4 minutes.

2 Add remaining ingredients except the cream (if using). Bring the mixture to a boil over high heat, reduce the heat to medium and simmer for 15 minutes.

3 Thicken with the cream (if using), or, if the soup is too thick, thin it by adding more apple juice.

Last Halloween, Little Kenny garnished each bowl of this spooky soup with apple.

Little Kenny's mother helps him peel, core and chop the apple and chop the onion and thyme.

Fabulous Mushroom and Pineapple Pita Pizza

Bone Rating:

Makes: 2 servings

Preparation Time:
  10 minutes

Cooking Time: 15 minutes

Cookware: Baking sheet

1	pita bread	1
1/4 cup	tomato sauce	60 mL
1 cup	sliced mushrooms	250 mL
1/2 cup	cubed pineapple	125 mL
2/3 cup	shredded mozzarella cheese	160 mL

There are thousands of different varieties of mushrooms. The most common are white or button mushrooms, but you can also experiment with portobello and shiitake mushrooms.

You can replace the pineapple with sliced pear or use mango for a pizza your friends and family will crave. Chopped fresh herbs, such as basil, and a touch of garlic can really make a difference in a plain tomato sauce. Try it and see what you think!

1. Place the pita bread on the baking sheet and distribute the tomato sauce evenly on top with a spoon.

2. Add the mushrooms and pineapple and sprinkle the cheese on top.

3. Bake the pita pizza in a preheated oven at 325°F (160°C) for 15 minutes, or until the cheese bubbles and browns slightly. Allow to cool for 2 to 3 minutes before serving.

Little Kenny's mother preheats the oven and helps him slice the mushrooms, cube the pineapple and shred the cheese.

Pineapples are a good source of vitamins A and C, but I like pineapples for their sweet natural flavor.

Potato and Onion Pizza

1	small pita or focaccia bread or pizza shell	1
1/4 cup	pesto sauce	60 mL
1	medium potato, cooked and thinly sliced	1
1	small onion, thinly sliced	1
2/3 cup	shredded mozzarella cheese	160 mL

Bone Rating:

Makes: 2 servings

Preparation Time:
   10 minutes

Cooking Time: 15 minutes

Cookware: Baking sheet

1 Place the bread or pizza shell on the baking sheet and distribute the pesto sauce evenly on top with a spoon.

2 Add the sliced potato and onion and sprinkle the cheese on top.

3 Bake in a preheated oven at 325°F (160°C) for 15 minutes, or until the cheese bubbles and browns slightly. Allow to cool for 2 to 3 minutes before serving.

Little Kenny's mother preheats the oven and helps him slice the potato and the onion and shred the cheese.

To lower the fat content of this recipe, use low-fat mozzarella cheese.

117

Fall Bell Pepper Sauté

Bell peppers come in red, yellow and green, but on occasion you can even find ones that are bright purple. Wow!

Bone Rating:

Makes: 4 to 6 servings

Preparation Time:
   10 minutes

Cooking Time: 15 minutes

Cookware: Large sauté pan

1/2 cup	vegetable stock or apple juice	125 mL
2	cloves garlic, chopped	2
2	large red bell peppers, thinly sliced	2
1	large green bell pepper, thinly sliced	1
1	large yellow bell pepper, thinly sliced	1
1/2 tsp	black pepper	2 mL
1/2 tsp	dried sage	2 mL
	or	
1 tbsp	chopped fresh sage	15 mL
1/2 tsp	sea salt	2 mL
1/4 cup	chopped fresh parsley	60 mL

Little Kenny's mother helps him chop the garlic, sage and parsley and slice the bell peppers.

1. In the sauté pan, heat the vegetable stock or apple juice over medium heat and gently sauté the garlic and bell peppers for 3 to 4 minutes.

2. Add the black pepper, sage and salt and sauté for another 2 minutes.

3. Mix in the parsley. Serve this flavorful sauté on top of salads or as a side dish.

To make bell pepper relish, finely chop the bell peppers and cook in 1 cup (250 mL) apple juice until the juice is reduced by one-quarter of the original amount. This should take about 15 minutes. The relish is delicious served over grilled foods.

Mexican Fried Rice Little Kenny Style

Bone Rating:

Makes: 4 servings

Preparation Time:
  10 minutes

Cooking Time: 15 minutes

Cookware: Wok or large
  sauté pan

1/2 cup	vegetable stock	125 mL
2	cloves garlic, chopped	2
1	small onion, chopped	1
1	small red bell pepper, sliced	1
2 cups	cooked long-grain white rice	500 mL
1/4 cup	chopped fresh coriander	60 mL
1/4 cup	mild salsa	60 mL
1/4 cup	soy sauce	60 mL
1/2 tsp	chili powder	2 mL

To lower the salt content of this recipe, use low-sodium soy sauce.

120

1. In the wok or sauté pan, heat the vegetable stock over high heat and stir-fry the garlic, onion and red bell pepper for about 2 to 3 minutes.

2. Add the rice, reduce the heat to medium and continue to stir-fry for 3 to 4 minutes.

3. Add remaining ingredients and stir-fry for 3 to 4 minutes.

Little Kenny's mother cooks the rice and helps him chop the garlic, onion, and coriander and slice the bell pepper.

For a much milder flavor, replace the coriander with fresh parsley. Remember, when cooking rice, cook 1 cup (250 mL) long-grain white rice in 2 cups (500 mL) water.

Penne with Garlic and Fresh Herbs

Little Kenny's mother cooks the pasta and drains it and helps him chop the garlic, bell peppers, onion, basil, thyme and parsley.

Pasta is a starchy product, but it is low in fat and supplies a moderate amount of protein.

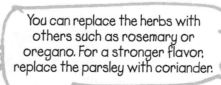

You can replace the herbs with others such as rosemary or oregano. For a stronger flavor, replace the parsley with coriander.

2 cups	penne (pasta tubes)	500 mL
2 tbsp	olive oil	30 mL
3	cloves garlic, finely chopped	3
1	medium green bell pepper, finely chopped	1
1	medium red bell pepper, finely chopped	1
1	small onion, finely chopped	1
1 cup	vegetable stock	250 mL
1/2 tsp	black pepper	2 mL
1/2 tsp	dried basil	2 mL
	or	
2 tbsp	finely chopped fresh basil	30 mL
1/2 tsp	dried thyme	2 mL
	or	
1 tsp	finely chopped fresh thyme	5 mL
1/2 tsp	sea salt	2 mL
1/2 cup	finely chopped fresh parsley	125 mL

Bone Rating:

Makes: 4 servings

Preparation Time:

10 minutes

Cooking Time: 20 minutes

Cookware: Large pot, large mixing bowl, sauté pan

There are three main types of garlic grown in North America today—American garlic, which has white skin, and Mexican and Italian garlic, which both have purple skin. Each has a distinct flavor. Elephant garlic, which is not really garlic but a member of the leek family, is larger than the three types of garlic and milder in flavor.

1 In the pot, cook the penne in boiling water for 7 to 8 minutes, or until the pasta is only slightly firm. Rinse the pasta with cold water to prevent it from cooking further, drain it and place it in the bowl. Toss the pasta with the olive oil and set aside.

2 In the sauté pan, combine all of the other ingredients, except the parsley. Sauté for about 10 minutes on medium heat, or until the liquid is reduced by half.

3 Stir in the penne and parsley and mix for 1 minute before serving.

Rotini with Chickpeas and Tomatoes

Rotini is a corkscrew-shaped pasta. Little Kenny loves all of the different shapes of pasta.

Little Kenny's mother cooks and drains the pasta and helps him chop the garlic, onion, parsley and basil.

Bone Rating:

Makes: 4 servings

Preparation Time:
   10 minutes

Cooking Time: 15 minutes

Cookware: Large pot,
   medium mixing bowl,
   sauté pan

2 cups	rotini (spiral pasta)	500 mL
2 tbsp	olive oil	30 mL
2	cloves garlic, chopped	2
1	small onion, chopped	1
1 cup	cooked or canned chickpeas, rinsed and drained	250 mL
1 cup	canned diced tomatoes	250 mL
1/2 cup	tomato juice	125 mL
1/2 tsp	black pepper	2 mL
1/2 cup	chopped fresh parsley	125 mL
1/2 tsp	dried basil	2 mL
	or	
2 tbsp	chopped fresh basil	30 mL
1/2 tsp	sea salt	2 mL

Chickpeas are high in fiber, low in fat and sodium (salt) and a rich source of the vitamins and minerals Little Kenny needs to help him grow.

You can replace the tomato juice with vegetable stock.

1 In the pot, cook the rotini in boiling water for 7 to 8 minutes, or until the pasta is only slightly firm. Rinse the pasta with cold water to prevent it from cooking further, drain it and place it in the bowl. Toss the pasta with the olive oil and set aside.

2 In the sauté pan, combine the remaining ingredients and simmer on medium heat for 8 to 10 minutes, or until the liquid is reduced by half.

3 Add the rotini and toss in the sauce for 1 minute before serving.

125

Thanksgiving Portobello Stir-fry

Bone Rating: 🦴🦴

Makes: 4 servings

Preparation Time:

10 minutes

Cooking Time: 10 minutes

Cookware: Sauté pan

At Thanksgiving, families gather together and eat quite a lot of food. Of course, there are always leftovers. Leftover vegetables or meats can be thrown into a stir-fry. Toss in the leftovers just before the end of the cooking to warm them up. Everyone will say "Wow!" to your new creation. It's best to use leftover vegetables that are still a little firm.

1/2 cup	vegetable stock	125 mL
4	large portobello mushroom caps, cleaned and cut into 1/2-inch (1-cm) strips	4
1	medium apple, peeled, cored and sliced	1
1	small onion, peeled and sliced	1
1/4 cup	apple juice	60 mL
1/4 cup	maple syrup	60 mL
1/4 cup	soy sauce	60 mL
1/2 tsp	black pepper	2 mL
1/2 tsp	sea salt	2 mL
1/4 tsp	cinnamon	1 mL

1. Heat the vegetable stock in the pan over high heat and gently sauté the mushrooms, apple and onion for about 5 minutes, stirring constantly.

2. Make a well in the center of the ingredients in the pan, reduce the heat to medium and add the remaining ingredients. Mix thoroughly and cook for another 4 minutes. Serve.

Little Kenny's mother helps him clean and cut the mushrooms into strips and peel, core and slice the apple and slice the onion.

Let's not forget that Thanksgiving is a time we also share with people outside of our families. Give to your local food bank at Thanksgiving to really make someone else smile.

Tofu Lo Mein

Lo Mein is a noodle dish that is stir-fried with a variety of ingredients. Use your imagination to see what exciting Lo Mein dishes you can create.

Little Kenny's mother cooks and drains the pasta, and helps him chop the garlic, mushrooms, ginger and green onions and cube the tofu.

Bone Rating:

Makes: 4 servings

Preparation Time: 10 minutes

Cooking Time: 15 minutes

Cookware: Large pot, medium mixing bowl, sauté pan

1/2 lb	spaghetti	250 g
2 tbsp	olive oil	30 mL
1/2 cup	vegetable stock	125 mL
1 tbsp	sesame oil	15 mL
2	cloves garlic, chopped	2
2 cups	chopped button mushrooms	500 mL
1 lb	firm tofu, cut into 1-inch (2.5-cm) cubes and patted dry	500 g
1/4 cup	soy sauce	60 mL
1 tbsp	chopped fresh ginger	15 mL
1 tsp	sugar	5 mL
1/2 cup	chopped green onions	125 mL

1 In the pot, cook the spaghetti in boiling water for 7 to 8 minutes, or until the pasta is only slightly firm. Rinse the pasta with cold water to prevent it from cooking further, drain it and place it in the bowl. Toss the pasta with the olive oil. Set aside.

2 In the sauté pan, heat the vegetable stock with the sesame oil over medium heat and sauté the garlic, mushrooms and tofu for 4 to 5 minutes. Add the soy sauce, ginger and sugar and cook for another 5 minutes.

3 Stir in the pasta and green onions and serve.

Fall Apple Crisp

Bone Rating: 🦴🦴

Makes: 6 to 8 servings

Preparation Time:
10 minutes

Cooking Time: 30 minutes

Cookware: Small and
medium mixing bowls,
greased 9-inch (2.5 L)
baking dish or pie plate

5 cups	peeled, cored and sliced apple	1.25 L
1/2 cup	apple juice	125 mL
2 tbsp	brown sugar	30 mL
1 1/2 tsp	lemon juice	7 mL
1 1/2 cups	quick-cooking rolled oats	325 mL
3/4 cup	brown sugar	175 mL
1/2 cup	melted butter	125 mL
1/2 cup	flour	125 mL
1 tsp	cinnamon	5 mL
1/2 tsp	sea salt	2 mL

To lower the fat content, use margarine instead of butter.

Try serving this crisp with whipping cream or even vanilla ice cream. Yum.

1 Place the apples in the baking dish or pie plate. In the small bowl, mix the apple juice, sugar and lemon juice. Combine the juice mixture with the apples to prevent them from browning.

Little Kenny's mother preheats the oven and helps him peel, core and slice the apples.

2 In the medium bowl, mix all of the other ingredients together. Cover the apples with the oats mixture.

3 Bake the crisp in a preheated oven at 375°F (190°C) for 30 minutes, or until the apples are tender. Serve warm or cold.

Replace the apples with pears or peaches.

Maple Syrup Bread Pudding

Bone Rating:

Makes: 4 to 6 servings

Preparation Time:

   10 minutes

Cooking Time: 30 minutes

Cookware: Small and large

   mixing bowls, nonstick

   13- × 9-inch (3.5 L)

   baking dish

3	medium eggs	3
2 cups	milk	500 mL
2 tbsp	brown sugar	30 mL
1 tsp	vanilla extract	5 mL
1/2 tsp	cinnamon	2 mL
8	slices white bread, torn into pieces	8
1/2 cup	maple syrup	125 mL
1/2 cup	raisins	125 mL

❶ In the small mixing bowl, combine all of the ingredients, except the bread, maple syrup and raisins. Mix well.

❷ Place the bread in the large mixing bowl and combine it with the egg mixture. Place the batter in the baking dish and pack down.

❸ Sprinkle the maple syrup and raisins on top of the batter. Bake the pudding in a preheated oven at 350°F (180°C) for 30 minutes.

Little Kenny's mother preheats the oven.

In this recipe, you can use bread that is more than a day old.

133

Winter

Little Kenny's Sunday Morning French Toast / 136

Little Kenny's Scrambled Eggs with Fresh Herbs / 138

Multi-Bean Salad with Fresh Parsley / 140

Little Kenny's Vegetable Chowder / 142

Minestrone Soup with Basil and Parmesan / 144

Potato and Leek Soup with Chili / 146

Carrot and Orange Quesadillas / 148

Spinach and Apple Pizza with Fresh Basil / 150

Heartwarming Zucchini Shepherd's Pie / 152

Hearty Mushroom and Onion Pie with Cheddar Cheese / 154

Helen's Homemade Macaroni and Cheese with Fresh Parsley / 156

Sweet Red Pepper Penne with Pineapple and Parsley / 158

Valentine Bow Tie Pasta with Tomatoes and Mozzarella / 160

Stir-Fried Portobello Mushrooms with Feta / 162

Creamy Garlic Mashed Potatoes With Thyme / 164

Winter Stir-fried Tofu with Apple and Cinnamon / 166

Carrot and Raisin Christmas Cake / 168

Chocolate Puffed Wheat Cake / 170

Little Kenny's Christmas Shortbread / 172

Little Kenny's Sunday Morning French Toast

French toast is usually served with maple syrup, but you can also serve it with preserves or jam.

For added flavor, use sliced raisin bread.

Little Kenny's mother sleeps in on Sunday mornings and wakes up to the delightful aroma of French toast.

4	medium eggs	4
1/4 cup	milk	60 mL
2 tbsp	brown sugar	30 mL
1/2 tsp	cinnamon	2 mL
4	slices bread	4
2 tbsp	butter	30 mL
	Maple syrup	

Bone Rating:

Makes: 4 servings

Preparation Time:

10 minutes

Cooking Time: 15 minutes

Cookware: Medium mixing

bowl, sauté pan

1 In the bowl, whisk together all of the ingredients, except the bread, butter and maple syrup.

2 Dip the bread slices one at a time into the egg mixture, making sure that it completely covers the bread and soaks in a little. Set the dipped bread slices aside on a plate in preparation for cooking them.

3 In the pan, melt the butter over medium heat. Cook the bread slices in the butter until they are lightly browned, about 3 to 4 minutes on each side. Serve the French toast warm with maple syrup.

Little Kenny's Scrambled Eggs with Fresh Herbs

Use any type of fresh herbs, such as oregano or rosemary. Dijon mustard is the "secret ingredient" in these scrambled eggs.

To lower the fat content of this recipe, use skim milk instead of table cream.

Little Kenny's mother helps him chop the fresh chives, basil and thyme.

Bone Rating:

Makes: 4 servings

Preparation Time:
   5 minutes

Cooking Time: 10 minutes

Cookware: Medium mixing bowl, sauté pan

6	medium eggs	6
1/2 cup	table cream	125 mL
1 tbsp	Dijon mustard	15 mL
2 tbsp	chopped fresh chives	30 mL
1 tsp	chopped fresh basil	5 mL
1 tsp	chopped fresh thyme	5 mL
1/2 tsp	black pepper	2 mL
1/2 tsp	sea salt	2 mL
2 tbsp	butter	30 mL

At your local supermarket, you'll find that eggs come in all sizes—from small to jumbo—as well as two colors, white and brown.

1 In the bowl, whisk together all of the ingredients, except the butter.

2 In the sauté pan, melt the butter over medium heat until it starts to bubble. Add the egg mixture and, using a spatula, scramble the eggs till they are firm and fluffy.

Multi-Bean Salad with Fresh Parsley

Little Kenny's mother helps him chop the bell pepper, onion and fresh parsley.

1 cup	canned black beans, drained	250 mL
1 cup	canned chickpeas, drained	250 mL
1 cup	canned red kidney beans, drained	250 mL
1 cup	canned white beans, drained	250 mL
1	small red bell pepper, chopped	1
1	small red onion, chopped	1
3/4 cup	chopped fresh parsley	180 mL
1/2 cup	apple cider vinegar	125 mL
1/2 cup	olive oil	125 mL
1/4 cup	apple juice	60 mL
2 tbsp	liquid honey	30 mL
1/2 tsp	black pepper	2 mL
1/2 tsp	sea salt	2 mL

Bone Rating:

Makes: 6 to 8 servings

Preparation Time:

15 minutes

Cookware: Large and small
mixing bowls

1 Rinse the black beans, chickpeas, kidney beans and white beans with cold water. In the large bowl, combine the beans and chickpeas with the bell pepper, onion and parsley and mix well.

2 In the small bowl, combine the vinegar, olive oil, apple juice, honey, black pepper and salt and whisk well.

3 Add the dressing to the bean mixture and mix well.

Replace the black beans with canned lentils. You can also replace the fresh parsley with 1/2 cup (125 mL) fresh coriander.

All of the beans used in this salad can also be used in a flavorful chili.

Beans are a wonderful source of protein, so Little Kenny has this salad quite often for lunch.

Little Kenny's Vegetable Chowder

Bone Rating:

Makes: 6 to 8 servings

Preparation Time:
   10 minutes

Cooking Time: 20 minutes

Cookware: Large pot

Little Kenny's mother helps him chop the celery, bell pepper, carrot and onion and dice the potato.

> This is a great recipe for using up leftover vegetables. Little Kenny always looks in the fridge to see what he can use in this chowder.

1/2 cup	vegetable stock	125 mL
1	celery stalk, chopped	1
1	green or red bell pepper, chopped	1
1	large carrot, chopped	1
1	small onion, chopped	1
1	potato, peeled and diced	1
5 cups	vegetable stock	1.25 L
1 cup	canned crushed tomatoes	250 mL
1/2 tsp	black pepper	2 mL
1/2 tsp	dried basil	2 mL
1/2 tsp	sea salt	2 mL
1 cup	table cream	250 mL

❶ Heat the vegetable stock in the pot over medium heat and sauté the celery, bell pepper, carrot and onion for about 2 minutes.

❷ Add all of the other ingredients, except the cream. Bring to a boil over high heat, reduce the heat to medium and simmer the soup for about 15 minutes.

❸ Add the cream and simmer for another 3 to 5 minutes, taking care not to boil the soup.

Minestrone Soup with Basil and Parmesan

Bone Rating:

Makes: 6 to 8 servings

Preparation Time:
  10 minutes

Cooking Time: 20 minutes

Cookware: Large pot

> Minestrone is an Italian soup that contains grated cheese and vegetables, pasta and sometimes beans.

1	celery stalk, chopped	1
1	small green bell pepper, chopped	1
1	small onion, chopped	1
1/4 cup	shredded carrot	60 mL
6 cups	vegetable stock	1.5 L
1 cup	macaroni	250 mL
1 cup	canned crushed or diced tomatoes	250 mL
2 tbsp	chopped fresh basil	30 mL
1/2 tsp	black pepper	2 mL
1/2 tsp	dried basil	2 mL
1/2 tsp	sea salt	2 mL
1/2 cup	grated Parmesan cheese	125 mL

1. Combine all of the ingredients in the pot, except the cheese.

2. Bring to a boil over high heat, immediately reduce the heat to medium and simmer the soup for about 15 minutes.

3. Add the cheese and mix well.

Little Kenny's mother helps him chop the celery, bell pepper, onion and fresh basil, shred the carrot and grate the cheese.

To lower the fat content of this recipe, use low-fat vegetable stock and low-fat Parmesan cheese.

Replace the macaroni with another type of pasta such as bow tie or shell pasta, or even fine egg noodles.

Potato and Leek Soup with Chili

Bone Rating:

Makes: 4 to 6 servings

Preparation Time:
   10 minutes

Cooking Time: 20 minutes

Cookware: Large pot,
   hand blender

Leeks are a member of the onion family and are especially flavorful in soups and stews.

1/2 cup	vegetable stock	125 mL
4	large leeks, washed, trimmed and sliced	4
2	large potatoes, peeled and cut into pieces	2
6 cups	vegetable stock	1.5 L
1 tsp	chili powder	5 mL
1/2 tsp	black pepper	2 mL
1/2 tsp	dried basil	2 mL
1/2 tsp	sea salt	2 mL
1/2 cup	table cream	125 mL

1 In the pot, heat the vegetable stock over medium heat and gently sauté the leeks till they are reduced by about half.

2 Add all of the other ingredients, except the cream. Bring to a boil over high heat, reduce the heat to medium and simmer the soup for about 15 minutes.

3 Using the hand blender, gently purée the soup until it has a nice smooth texture. Add the table cream and simmer the soup over medium heat for another 2 minutes.

Little Kenny's mother helps him trim and cut the leeks into slices and peel and cut the potatoes into pieces.

To lower the fat content of this recipe, use low-fat vegetable stock and skim milk instead of cream.

Replace the chili powder with a mild curry powder to give the soup a completely different flavor.

Carrot and Orange Quesadillas

A Mexican dish, quesadillas are usually served as an appetizer and can be made with different fillings. Little Kenny uses leftovers to make a variety of quesadillas.

Bone Rating:

Makes: 2 servings

Preparation Time:
   10 minutes

Cooking Time: 10 minutes

Cookware: Small mixing
   bowl, baking sheet

1	small orange, peeled, seeded and chopped	1
1/2 cup	shredded carrot	125 mL
2 tbsp	orange marmalade	30 mL
3/4 cup	shredded Monterey Jack cheese	180 mL
2 tbsp	soft butter	30 mL
4	small flour tortillas	4

Little Kenny's mother preheats the oven and helps him peel and chop the orange and shred the carrot and cheese.

To lower the fat content of this recipe, use low-fat mozzarella instead of Monterey Jack cheese.

Replace the orange with a chopped pear and use pear preserves instead of the marmalade.

1 In the bowl, combine the orange, carrot, marmalade and cheese. Mix well.

2 Butter 2 tortillas and place them buttered side down on the baking sheet. Fill each tortilla evenly with the orange mixture. Place a tortilla on top of each filled tortilla and butter the top.

3 Bake the tortillas in a preheated oven at 325°F (160°C) for about 10 to 12 minutes. Cut the tortillas in half before serving.

Spinach and Apple Pizza with Fresh Basil

Bone Rating:

Makes: 2 servings

Preparation Time:
   10 minutes

Cooking Time: 15 minutes

Cookware: Baking sheet

Little Kenny's mother preheats the oven and helps him chop the spinach and fresh basil, peel, core and slice the apple, slice the onion and shred the cheese.

1	small premade or frozen pizza shell	1
1/2 cup	apple sauce	125 mL
1 1/2 cups	chopped spinach	375 mL
1	medium apple, peeled, cored and thinly sliced	1
1/2	small onion, sliced	1/2
1/2 cup	shredded mozzarella cheese	125 mL
2 tbsp	chopped fresh basil	30 mL

1 Place the pizza shell on the baking sheet and evenly distribute the apple sauce on top.

2 Add the spinach, then the apple and onion and top with the cheese and fresh basil.

3 Bake the pizza in a preheated oven at 325°F (160°C) for about 15 minutes, or until the cheese is bubbling. Allow the pizza to cool until it is just warm. Slice into 4 pieces and serve.

Heartwarming Zucchini Shepherd's Pie

Bone Rating: 🦴🦴🦴

Makes: 4 to 6 servings

Preparation Time: 15 minutes

Cooking Time: 20 minutes

Cookware: Large pot, potato masher, sauté pan, 8-inch (2 L) cake pan or casserole dish

4	large potatoes, peeled and chopped	4
1/2 cup	cream	125 mL
2 tbsp	butter	30 mL
1/2 cup	apple juice	125 mL
2	stalks celery, chopped	2
1	small onion, chopped	1
3 cups	chopped mushrooms	750 mL
3 cups	chopped zucchini	750 mL
1/2 tsp	chili powder	2 mL
1/2 tsp	black pepper	2 mL
1/2 tsp	sea salt	2 mL
1 cup	shredded Cheddar cheese	250 mL

When you buy zucchini, make sure that the skin is free of blemishes and has a nice bright color.

Zucchini is a popular summer squash available all year long at your local supermarket.

1. In the pot, cook the potatoes in boiling water until they are tender. Drain the potatoes and return them to the pot. Add the cream and butter and mash the potatoes until they are fluffy.

2. Heat the apple juice in the pan over medium heat. Add all the other ingredients, except the cheese, and sauté the mixture for about 3 minutes.

3. Place the vegetable mixture in the cake pan or casserole dish. Top with the mashed potatoes and then the cheese. Bake the pie in a preheated oven at 375°F (190°C) for 15 minutes. Allow the pie to cool slightly before cutting it.

Little Kenny's mother preheats the oven and helps him peel, chop, boil and drain the potatoes, chop the celery, onion, mushrooms and zucchini and shred the cheese.

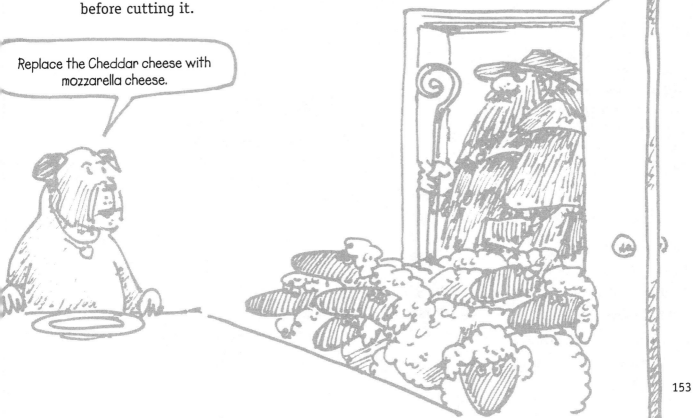

Replace the Cheddar cheese with mozzarella cheese.

Hearty Mushroom and Onion Pie with Cheddar Cheese

To lower the fat content of this recipe, use low-fat Cheddar cheese.

Little Kenny's mother preheats the oven and helps him chop the garlic, celery, onion, mushrooms and fresh thyme and shred the carrot and cheese.

Bone Rating:

Makes: 4 to 6 servings

Preparation Time:
   10 minutes

Cooking Time: 20 minutes

Cookware: Large sauté pan

1/2 cup	vegetable stock	125 mL
2	cloves garlic, finely chopped	2
2	stalks celery, finely chopped	2
1	medium onion, finely chopped	1
6 cups	finely chopped mushrooms	1.5 L
1/2 cup	shredded carrot	125 mL
1/2 tsp	chili powder	2 mL
1/2 tsp	black pepper	2 mL
1/2 tsp	dried thyme	2 mL
	or	
1 tbsp	chopped fresh thyme	15 mL
1/2 tsp	sea salt	2 mL
3/4 cup	shredded mild Cheddar cheese	180 mL
1	9-inch (23 cm) frozen pie shell	1

This is Little Kenny's version of a classic French mushroom and onion pie. He quite often makes this recipe in advance and just warms the pie up before serving it.

1. In the sauté pan, heat the vegetable stock over medium heat and sauté the garlic, celery and onion for about 3 minutes.

2. Add the mushrooms, carrot, chili powder, black pepper, thyme and salt. Sauté the mixture for about 8 to 10 minutes.

3. Add cheese and mix well. Spread the mixture evenly in the pie shell. Bake the pie in a preheated oven at 375°F (190°C) for 15 minutes. Allow the pie to cool slightly before cutting.

Mushrooms, mushrooms, mushrooms. Little Kenny likes to use button mushrooms, but you can find other varieties, such as portobello, shiitake or cremini mushrooms, at your local supermarket.

155

Helen's Homemade Macaroni and Cheese with Fresh Parsley

Bone Rating:

Makes: 4 servings

Preparation Time:
10 minutes

Cooking Time: 15 minutes

Cookware: Large pot

Little Kenny's mother boils and drains the pasta and helps him shred the cheese and chop the fresh parsley.

2 cups	macaroni	500 mL
1 cup	shredded mild Cheddar cheese	250 mL
3/4 cup	milk	180 mL
1 tbsp	butter	15 mL
1 tbsp	Dijon mustard	15 mL
1/2 tsp	sea salt	2 mL
1/2 cup	chopped fresh parsley	125 mL

1. In the pot, cook the pasta in boiling water for 7 to 8 minutes. Drain the pasta and return it to the pot.

2. Add all of the other ingredients, except the parsley. Cook on medium heat until the cheese has melted and the sauce is smooth.

3. Add the fresh parsley and serve the pasta warm.

To lower the fat content of this recipe, replace the milk with nonfat or skim milk and the Cheddar cheese with low-fat Cheddar cheese.

Sweet Red Pepper Penne with Pineapple and Parsley

Bone Rating:

Makes: 4 servings

Preparation Time:
   10 minutes

Cooking Time: 15 minutes

Cookware: Large pot, large
   sauté pan

Little Kenny's mother boils and drains *the* pasta and helps him slice *the* bell peppers and onion, cube *the* pineapple and chop *the* fresh parsley and thyme.

2 1/2 cups	penne (pasta tubes)	625 mL
3/4 cup	pineapple juice	180 mL
2	large red bell peppers, sliced	2
1	small red onion, thinly sliced	1
1/2 cup	cubed pineapple	125 mL
1/4 cup	chopped fresh parsley	60 mL
1/2 tsp	black pepper	2 mL
1/2 tsp	dried thyme	2 mL
	or	
1 tbsp	chopped fresh thyme	15 mL
1/2 tsp	sea salt	2 mL

1 In the pot, cook the pasta in boiling water. Drain the pasta and set it aside.

2 In the sauté pan, bring the pineapple juice to a boil over high heat. Add all of the other ingredients, reduce the heat to medium and simmer for 5 minutes.

3 Add the pasta to the sauce and mix well. Serve warm.

Christopher Columbus found red peppers during his travels in the Americas and took some back to Spain. Red peppers are featured in a lot of Spanish cooking.

Valentine Bow Tie Pasta with Tomatoes and Mozzarella

Replace the mozzarella with feta or mild goat cheese.

Little Kenny made this recipe for Valentine's Day for his parents. They loved it.

2 cups	bow tie pasta	500 mL
1 cup	canned crushed or diced tomatoes	250 mL
1/2 cup	shredded mozzarella cheese	125 mL
2 tbsp	balsamic vinegar	30 mL
1/2 tsp	black pepper	2 mL
1/2 tsp	sea salt	2 mL
1/2 cup	chopped fresh basil	125 mL

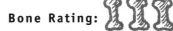

Bone Rating:

Makes: 4 servings

Preparation Time:
   10 minutes

Cooking Time: 15 minutes

Cookware: Large pot

1 In the pot, cook the pasta in boiling water for 7 to 8 minutes. Drain the pasta and set it aside.

2 Place all of the other ingredients in the pot, except the fresh basil. Cook the tomato mixture on low heat for about 3 to 5 minutes.

3 Return the pasta to the pot, add the fresh basil and mix well. Cook for another 2 to 3 minutes. Serve warm.

Little Kenny's mother boils and drains the pasta and helps him shred the cheese and chop the fresh basil.

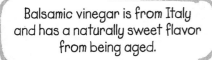

Balsamic vinegar is from Italy and has a naturally sweet flavor from being aged.

Stir-fried Portobello Mushrooms with Feta

Bone Rating: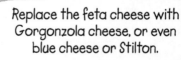

Makes 4

Preparation Time:
   10 minutes

Cooking Time: 10 minutes

Cookware: Sauté pan

1/2 cup	apple juice	125 mL
1	small onion, sliced	1
4	medium portobello mushrooms, cleaned and sliced	4
1	small red bell pepper, sliced lengthwise	1
1/4 cup	sliced olives (optional)	60 mL
1/2 tsp	dried rosemary	2 mL
	or	
1 tbsp	chopped fresh rosemary	15 mL
1/2 cup	crumbled feta cheese	125 mL

To clean the mushrooms caps, just rub them gently with a damp paper towel.

Replace the feta cheese with Gorgonzola cheese, or even blue cheese or Stilton.

1. Heat the apple juice in the pan on high heat and sauté the onion for about 2 minutes, or until tender.

2. Add the mushrooms, bell pepper, olives (if using) and rosemary, reduce the heat to medium and stir-fry another 7 to 8 minutes, or until the mushrooms are cooked.

3. Sprinkle the feta cheese on top and serve immediately

Little Kenny's mother helps him slice the onion, mushrooms and olives and chop the rosemary.

163

Creamy Garlic Mashed Potatoes with Thyme

Replace the fresh thyme with fresh basil, oregano or rosemary.

To lower the fat content of this recipe, use skim milk instead of table cream and use low-fat cream cheese.

Bone Rating:

Makes: 4 servings

Preparation Time: 10 Minutes

Cooking Time: 20 Minutes

Cookware: Large pot, potato masher

4	potatoes, peeled and cut into pieces	4
2	cloves garlic, finely chopped	2
1/2 cup	table cream	125 mL
2 tbsp	butter	30 mL
2 tbsp	cream cheese	30 mL
1 tbsp	finely chopped fresh thyme	15 mL
1/2 tsp	black pepper	2 mL
1/2 tsp	sea salt	2 mL

1. Place the potatoes in the pot with enough water to cover them. Bring to a boil on high heat, reduce the heat to medium and simmer the potatoes for about 15 to 20 minutes.

2. Drain the potatoes and place them back in the pot.

3. Mash the potatoes using the potato masher. Add all of the other ingredients and blend until the potatoes are fluffy and smooth.

Little Kenny's mother helps him peel cut, boil and drain the potatoes and chop the garlic and thyme.

Winter Stir-fried Tofu with Apple and Cinnamon

3/4 cup	apple juice	175 mL
1	medium apple, peeled, cored and sliced	1
1	small onion, chopped	1
1	small red bell pepper, sliced	1
1 lb	firm tofu, cut into 1/2-inch (1 cm) cubes and patted dry	500 g
1/2 tsp	dried basil or	2 mL
1 tbsp	chopped fresh basil	15 mL
1/2 cup	apple sauce	125 mL
2 tbsp	liquid honey	30 mL
1/2 tsp	cinnamon	2 mL

Bone Rating:

Makes: 4 servings

Preparation Time:
   10 minutes

Cooking Time: 10 minutes

Cookware: Sauté pan

Little Kenny's mother helps him peel, core and slice the apple, chop the onion and fresh basil, slice the bell pepper and cube the tofu.

1 In the pan, heat the apple juice over high heat and stir-fry the apple, onion and bell pepper for about 2 minutes.

2 Add the tofu and basil, reduce the heat to medium and stir-fry for another 5 to 6 minutes.

3 Make a hole in the center of the tofu mixture and add the applesauce, honey and cinnamon. Stir-fry for another 3 to 4 minutes, or until the sauce has coated the ingredients.

Replace the apple with pear and use pear nectar instead of apple sauce. A great addition would be 1/4 cup (60 mL) crumbled blue or Stilton cheese sprinkled on at the end of the stir-frying.

Tofu is made from soybeans and is usually found in two varieties, firm and soft. Firm tofu keeps its shape when you stir-fry it and soft tofu is good for scrambling like eggs.

Carrot and Raisin Christmas Cake

Bone Rating:

Makes: 10- × 6-inch
   (3 L) loaf

Preparation Time:
   10 minutes

Cooking Time: 1 hour

Cookware: Large and
   medium mixing bowl,
   nonstick 10- × 6-inch
   (3 L) loaf pan

> Little Kenny quite often gives this cake away wrapped nicely as a Christmas gift.

2 cups	brown sugar	500 mL
1 1/2 cups	canola oil	375 mL
4	small eggs	4
2 cups	chopped mixed candied fruit	500 mL
2 cups	shredded carrots	500 mL
2 cups	raisins	500 mL
1 cup	chopped walnuts	250 mL
1 tsp	vanilla extract	5 mL
3 cups	flour	750 mL
2 tsp	baking soda	10 mL
1 tbsp	baking powder	15 mL
1 tbsp	cinnamon	15 mL
1 tsp	sea salt	5 mL
1/2 tsp	cloves	2 mL

1. In the large bowl, combine the brown sugar and oil. Mix in the eggs, candied fruit, carrots, raisins, walnuts and vanilla.

2. In the medium bowl, sift together the flour, baking soda, baking powder, cinnamon, salt and cloves.

3. Add the flour mixture to the fruit mixture and mix until smooth. Pour the batter into the loaf pan and bake in a preheated oven at 325°F (160°C) for about 1 hour, or until a toothpick inserted in the center of the cake comes out clean.

Little Kenny's mother preheats the oven and helps him chop the candied fruit and walnuts and shred the carrots.

When this cake is baking, my nose works overtime.

You can replace the raisins in this recipe with chopped dates.

Chocolate Puffed Wheat Cake

Bone Rating:

Makes: 10- × 8-inch (2L) cake

Preparation Time: 10 minutes

Cooking Time: 10 minutes

Cookware: Medium pot, large mixing bowl, nonstick 10- × 8-inch (2 L) cake pan

Little Kenny's mother cooks and pours the marshmallow mixture and helps him mix it with the puffed wheat.

10	large marshmallows	10
1 cup	brown sugar	250 mL
1/2 cup	butter	125 mL
1/2 cup	corn syrup	125 mL
4 tbsp	cocoa	60 mL
1 tsp	vanilla extract	5 mL
1/4 tsp	cinnamon	1 mL
8 cups	puffed wheat cereal	2 L

1 In the pot, combine the marshmallows, brown sugar, butter, corn syrup and cocoa. Bring the marshmallow mixture to a boil and stir in the vanilla. Boil the mixture for about 4 to 5 minutes and remove it from the heat.

2 Place the puffed wheat in the bowl. Pour the marshmallow mixture over the puffed wheat (only an adult should do this) and mix until the cereal is evenly coated, making sure that you don't touch the hot marshmallow mixture.

3 Place the puffed wheat mixture in the cake pan and press down firmly with a spatula or the back of a spoon. Let the cake cool for at least 2 hours and cut into squares.

Little Kenny's Christmas Shortbread

1 cup	butter, softened	250 mL
1/2 cup	icing sugar	125 mL
1 1/2 cups	flour	375 mL
1/2 cup	chopped red and green candied cherries	125 mL

Bone Rating: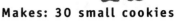

Makes: 30 small cookies

Preparation Time:
10 minutes

Cooking Time: 10 to 12 minutes

Cookware: Medium bowl, nonstick baking sheet

1 In the bowl, combine the butter and icing sugar and mix until smooth. Add the flour and mix until the ingredients are evenly combined.

2 Roll the dough into 1-inch (2 cm) balls and place them on the baking sheet. Press a piece of candied cherry gently into the center of each cookie.

3 Bake the cookies in a preheated oven at 350°F (180°C) for 10 to 12 minutes, or until the edges are lightly browned.

Little Kenny's mother preheats the oven and helps him chop the candied fruit.

I put out six cookies and milk last year for Santa.

Little Kenny's mother likes to make these cookies for her family and friends at Christmas.

index

A

APPLES
Fall Apple Crisp, 130–131
Spinach and Apple Pizza with Fresh Basil, 150–151
Spooky Halloween Pumpkin Soup with Apple, 112–113
Winter Stir-fried Tofu with Apple and Cinnamon, 166–167

Appliances, safety tips, 16–17

B

BASIL
Green Stir-fry with Basil, 48–49
Minestrone Soup with Basil and Parmesan, 144–145
Spinach and Apple Pizza with Fresh Basil, 150–151
Tomato and Basil Pizza with Goat Cheese on Phyllo, 80–81

BEANS
Mexican Beans and Rice with Coriander, 88–89
Multi-Bean Salad with Fresh Parsley, 140–141

BELL PEPPERS
Fall Bell Pepper Sauté, 118–119

The Best Western Sandwich with Herbs, 38–39

BLUEBERRIES
Blueberry Muffins Extraordinaire, 60–61

BRAN
Carrot and Bran Muffins with Raisins, 22–23
Little Kenny's Bran Muffins Fantastic, 101–101

BROCCOLI
Mother's Day Four-Cheese Rice and Broccoli, 42–43

BREAD (See also Pita)
The Best Western Sandwich with Herbs, 38–39

Focaccia Pizza with Olives and Feta, 78–79
Little Kenny's Sunday Morning French Toast, 136–137
Maple Syrup Bread Pudding, 132–133

C

CAKES (See also Cookies; Desserts; Pies)
Carrot and Raisin Christmas Cake, 168–169
Chocolate Puffed Wheat Cake, 170–171
Carrot and Bran Muffins with Raisins, 22–23
Carrot and Orange Quesadillas, 148–149
Carrot and Raisin Christmas Cake, 168–169
Fabulous Carrot Pancakes, 62–63
Spring Carrot and Orange Salad, 30–31

CHEESE
Carrot and Orange Quesadillas, 148–149
Cheesy Vegetable Stew, 82–83
Focaccia Pizza with Olives and Feta, 78–79
Hearty Mushroom and Onion Pie with Cheddar Cheese, 154–155
Helen's Homemade Macaroni and Cheese with Fresh Parsley, 156–157
Little Kenny's Mashed Potato Soup with Cheddar Cheese, 110–111
Minestrone Soup with Basil and Parmesan, 144–145
Mother's Day Four-Cheese Rice and Broccoli, 42–43
Mushroom Helper with Pasta and Cheese, 44–45
Scrambled Eggs with Onion, Parmesan and Red Pepper, 102–103
Sleepy Kenny's Wakeup Breakfast Soup, 104–105
Spinach and Pear Salad with Feta, 28–29
Spring Vegetables and Fusilli with Parmesan, 50–51

Stir-fried Portobello Mushrooms, 162–163
Tomato and Basil Pizza with Goat Cheese on Phyllo, 80–81
Valentine Bow Tie Pasta with Tomatoes and Mozzarella, 160–161
Cheesy Vegetable Stew, 82–83

CHICKPEAS
Rotini with Chickpeas and Tomatoes, 124–125

CHILI
Potato and Leek Soup with Chili, 146–147

Chilled Pineapple Soup with Yogurt and Mint, 72
Chilled Strawberry Soup with Thyme, 74–75

CHOCOLATE
Chocolate Puffed Wheat Cake, 170–171
Little Kenny's Unbelievable Chocolate Chip Cookies, 56–57

CINNAMON
Winter Stir-fried Tofu with Apple and Cinnamon, 166–167

cleanliness, tips

COOKIES
Incredible Peanut Butter Cookies, 54–55
Little Kenny's Christmas Shortbread, 172–173
Little Kenny's Unbelievable Chocolate Chip Cookies, 56–57

cooking terms, 18–19

CORIANDER
Mexican Beans and Rice with Coriander, 88–89

CORN
Very Creamy Cream of Corn and Potato Soup, 36–37

Couscous Salad with Raisins and Parsley Madness, 106–107
Creamy Garlic Mashed Potatoes with Thyme, 164–165

CURRY
Spaghetti Squash Curry, 46–47

D

DESSERTS (See also Cakes; Cookies; Pies–Sweet)
Fall Apple Crisp, 130–131
Long Weekend Apple-Peach Crisp, 96–97
Maple Syrup Bread Pudding, 132–133

E

EGGS
Lazy Summer Salsa Scrambled Eggs with Parsley, 64–65
Little Kenny's Scrambled Eggs with Fresh Herbs, 138–139
Scrambled Eggs with Onion, Parmesan and Red Pepper, 102–103

F

Fabulous Carrot Pancakes, 62–63
Fabulous Mushroom and Pineapple Pita Pizza, 114–115
Fall Apple Crisp, 130–131
Fall Bell Pepper Sauté, 118–119
Focaccia Pizza with Olives and Feta, 78–79
food preparation, safety tips, 15–17
French toast, 136–137
Fresh Fruit with Macaroni and Mint, 66–67

FRUIT
Fresh Fruit with Macaroni and Mint, 66–67
Fruit Pizza on Pita, 26–27

G

GARLIC
Creamy Garlic Mashed Potatoes with Thyme, 164–165
Penne with Garlic and Fresh Herbs, 122–123

Gazpacho with Fresh Herbs, 76–77
Greek Pasta with Spinach and Tomatoes, 74–85
Green Stir-fry with Basil, 48–49

Grilled Vegetable Salad with Balsamic Vinegar, 68–69

H
Heartwarming Zucchini Shepherd's Pie, 152–153
Hearty Mushroom and Onion Pie with Cheddar Cheese, 154–155
Helen's Easy Strawberry Pie, 94–95
Helen's Homemade Macaroni and Cheese with Fresh Parsley, 156–157

I
Incredible Peanut Butter Cookies, 54–55

K
kitchen safety, 15–17

L
Lazy Summer Salsa Scrambled Eggs with Parsley, 64–65

LEEKS
Potato and Leek Soup with Chili, 146

Little Kenny's Bran Muffins Fantastic, 100–101
Little Kenny's Christmas Shortbread, 172–173
Little Kenny's Easy Tomato and Rice Soup, 32–33
Little Kenny's Hotcakes, 24–25
Little Kenny's Mashed Potato Soup with Cheddar Cheese, 110–111
Little Kenny's Mighty Caesar Salad, 108–109
Little Kenny's Pad Thai, 52–53
Little Kenny's Scrambled Eggs with Fresh Herbs, 138
Little Kenny's Simple Spaghetti and Tomato Sauce, 86–87
Little Kenny's Sunday Morning French Toast, 136–137
Little Kenny's Unbelievable Chocolate Chip Cookies, 56–57
Little Kenny's Vegetable Chowder, 142–143
Long Weekend Apple-Peach Crisp, 96–97

M
Macaroni and cheese, 156–157
Maple Syrup Bread Pudding, 132–133
Mexican Beans and Rice with Coriander, 88–89
Mexican Fried Rice Little Kenny Style, 120–121
Mexican Stir-fry with Orange, 90–91
Minestrone Soup with Basil and Parmesan, 144–145

MINT
Chilled Pineapple Soup with Yogurt and Mint, 72–73
Fresh Fruit with Macaroni and Mint, 66–67
Mother's Day Four-Cheese Rice and Broccoli, 42–43

MUFFINS
Blueberry Muffins Extraordinaire, 60–61
Carrot and Bran Muffins with Raisins, 22–23
Little Kenny's Bran Muffins Fantastic, 100–101
Multi-Bean Salad with Fresh Parsley, 140–141

MUSHROOMS
Fabulous Mushroom and Pineapple Pita Pizza, 114–115
Hearty Mushroom and Onion Pie with Cheddar Cheese, 154–155
Mushroom Helper with Pasta and Cheese, 44–45
Portobello Mushroom Pizza with Red Pepper, 40–41
Stir-fried Portobello Mushrooms with Feta, 162–163
Thanksgiving Portobello Stir-fry, 126–127

O
ONIONS
Hearty Mushroom and Onion Pie with Cheddar Cheese, 154–155
Potato and Onion Pizza, 116–117
Scrambled Eggs with Onion, Parmesan and Red Pepper, 102–103

ORANGES
Carrot and Orange Quesadillas, 148–149
Mexican Stir-fry with Orange, 90–91
Spring Carrot and Orange Salad, 30–31
Original Stir-fry with Sesame Seeds, 92–93
Oven safety, 15

P
Pad Thai, 52–53

PANCAKES
Fabulous Carrot Pancakes, 62–63
Little Kenny's Hotcakes, 24–25

PARSLEY
Couscous Salad with Raisin and Parsley Madness, 106–107
Helen's Homemade Macaroni and Cheese with Fresh Parsley, 156–157
Lazy Summer Salsa Scrambled Eggs with Parsley, 64–65
Multi-Bean Salad with Fresh Parsley, 140–141
Spring Vegetable Soup with Fresh Parsley, 34–35
Sweet Red Pepper Penne with Pineapple and Parsley, 158–159

PASTA
Fresh Fruit with Macaroni and Mint, 66–67
Greek Pasta with Spinach and Tomatoes, 84–85
Helen's Homemade Macaroni and Cheese with Fresh Parsley, 156–157
Little Kenny's Simple Spaghetti and Tomato Sauce, 86–87
Minestrone Soup with Basil and Parmesan, 144–145
Mushroom Helper with Pasta and Cheese, 44–45
Penne with Garlic and Fresh Herbs, 122–123
Rotini with Chickpeas and Tomatoes, 124–125
Spring Vegetables and Fusilli with Parmesan, 50–51

Sweet Red Pepper Penne with Pineapple and Parsley, 158–159
Tofu Lo Mein, 128–129
Valentine Bow Tie Pasta with Tomatoes and Mozzarella, 160–161
Penne with Garlic and Fresh Herbs, 122–123

PIES–Sweet
Helen's Easy Strawberry Pie, 94–95

PIES–Savoury
Hearty Mushroom and Onion Pie with Cheddar Cheese, 154–155

PINEAPPLE
Fabulous Mushroom and Pineapple Pita Pizza, 114–115
Sweet Red Pepper Penne with Pineapple and Parsley, 158–159

PITA
Fabulous Mushroom and Pineapple Pita Pizza, 114–115
Fruit Pizza on Pita, 24–25

PIZZA
Fabulous Mushroom and Pineapple Pita Pizza, 114–115
Focaccia Pizza with Olives and Feta, 78–79
Fruit Pizza on Pita, 26–27
Portobello Mushroom Pizza with Red Pepper, 40–41
Potato and Onion Pizza, 116–117
Spinach and Apple Pizza with Fresh Basil, 150–151
Tomato and Basil Pizza with Goat Cheese on Phyllo, 80–81

Portobello Mushroom Pizza with Red Pepper, 40–41

POTATOES
Creamy Garlic Mashed Potatoes with Thyme, 164–165
Little Kenny's Mashed Potato Soup with Cheddar Cheese, 110–111
Potato and Leek Soup with Chili, 146–147
Potato and Onion Pizza, 116–117
Summer Potato Salad, 70–71
Very Creamy Cream of Corn and Potato Soup, 36–37

PUMPKIN
Spooky Halloween Pumpkin Soup
   with Apple, 112–113

Q
Quesadillas, 148–149

R
RAISINS
Carrot and Bran Muffins with
   Raisins, 22–23
Carrot and Raisin Christmas Cake,
   168–169
Couscous Salad with Raisin and
   Parsley Madness, 106–107

RED PEPPER
Portobello Mushroom Pizza with
   Red Pepper, 40–51
Scrambled Eggs with Onion,
   Parmesan and Red Pepper,
   102–103
Sweet Red Pepper Penne with
   Pineapple and Parsley, 158–159

RICE
Little Kenny's Easy Tomato and
   Rice Soup, 32–33
Mexican Beans and Rice with
   Coriander, 88–89
Mexican Fried Rice Little Kenny
   Style, 120–121
Mother's Day Four-Cheese Rice and
   Broccoli, 42–43

Rotini with Chickpeas and
   Tomatoes, 124–125

S
SALADS
Couscous Salad with Raisin and
   Parsley Madness, 106–107
Grilled Vegetable Salad with
   Balsamic Vinegar, 68–69
Little Kenny's Mighty Caesar
   Salad, 108–109
Multi-Bean Salad with Fresh
   Parsley, 140–141
Spinach and Pear Salad with Feta,
   28–29

Spring Carrot and Orange Salad,
   30–31
Summer Potato Salad, 70–71

SANDWICHES
The Best Western Sandwich with
   Herbs, 48–39

Scrambled Eggs with Onion,
   Parmesan and Red Pepper,
   102–103

SESAME SEEDS
Original Stir-fry with Sesame
   Seeds, 92–93

Shepherd's Pie, 152–53
Shortbread, 172–173
Sleepy Kenny's Wakeup Breakfast
   Soup, 104–105

SOUPS AND CHOWDER
Chilled Pineapple Soup with
   Yogurt and Mint, 72–73
Chilled Strawberry Soup with
   Thyme, 74–75
Gazpacho with Fresh Herbs, 76–77
Little Kenny's Easy Tomato and
   Rice Soup, 32–33
Little Kenny's Mashed Potato Soup
   with Cheddar Cheese, 110–111
Little Kenny's Vegetable Chowder,
   142–143
Minestrone Soup with Basil and
   Parmesan, 144–145
Potato and Leek Soup with Chili,
   146–147
Sleepy Kenny's Wakeup Breakfast
   Soup, 104–105
Spooky Haloween Pumpkin Soup
   with Apple, 112–113
Spring Vegetable Soup with Fresh
   Parsley, 34–35
Very Creamy Cream of Corn and
   Potato Soup, 36–37

Spaghetti Squash Curry, 46–47

SPINACH
Greek Pasta with Spinach and
   Tomatoes, 84–85
Spinach and Apple Pizza with
   Fresh Basil, 150–151

Spinach and Pear Salad with Feta,
   28–29
Spooky Halloween Pumpkin Soup
   with Apple, 112–113
Spring Vegetable Soup with Fresh
   Parsley, 34–35
Spring Vegetables and Fusilli with
   Parmesan, 50–51

SQUASH
Spaghetti Squash Curry, 46–47

STIR-FRIES
Green Stir-fry with Basil, 48–49
Mexican Stir-fry with Orange,
   90–91
Original Stir-fry with Sesame
   Seeds, 92–93
Stir-fried Portobello Mushrooms
   with Feta, 162–163
Thanksgiving Portobello Stir-fry,
   120–127
Winter Stir-fried Tofu with Apple
   and Cinnamon, 166–167

stove top safety, 17

STRAWBERRIES
Chilled Strawberry Soup with
   Thyme, 74–75
Helen's Easy Strawberry Pie, 94–95

Summer Potato Salad, 70–71
Sweet Red Pepper Penne with
   Pineapple and Parsley, 158–159
Thanksgiving Portobello Stir-fry,
   126–127

THYME
Chilled Strawberry Soup with
   Thyme, 74–75
Creamy Garlic Mashed Potatoes
   with Thyme, 164–165

TOFU
Tofu Lo Mein, 128–129
Winter Stir-fried Tofu with Apple
   and Cinnamon, 166–167

TOMATOES
Greek Pasta with Spinach and
   Tomatoes, 84–85

Little Kenny's Easy Tomato and
   Rice Soup, 32–33
Little Kenny's Simple Spaghetti
   and Tomato Sauce, 86–87
Rotini with Chickpeas and
   Tomatoes, 124–125
Tomato and Basil Pizza with Goat
   Cheese on Phyllo, 80–81
Valentine Bow Tie Pasta with
   Tomatoes and Mozzarella,
   160–161

V
Valentine Bow Tie Pasta with
   Tomatoes and Mozzarella,
   160–161

VEGETABLES
Cheesy Vegetable Stew, 82–83
Gazpacho with Fresh Herbs, 76–77
Green Stir-fry with Basil, 48–49
Grilled Vegetable Salad with
   Balsamic Vinegar, 68–69
Little Kenny's Vegetable Chowder,
   142–143
Mexican Stir-fry with Orange,
   90–91
Original Stir-fry with Sesame
   Seeds, 92–93
Spring Vegetable Soup with Fresh
   Parsley, 34
Spring Vegetables and Fusilli with
   Parmesan, 50–51
Very Creamy Cream of Corn and
   Potato Soup, 36–37

W
Winter Stir-fried Tofu with Apple
   and Cinnamon, 166–167

Y
YOGURT
Chilled Pineapple Soup with
   Yogurt and Mint, 72–73

Z
ZUCCHINI
Heartwarming Zucchini Shepherd's
   Pie, 152–153